Ghost Hunting in Kentucky and Beyond

Experience the Unexplained

by

Patti Starr

Certified Ghost Hunter

In Loving Memory of

My mom, Eunice Nabors, and my dad, Bill Russell

International Standard Book Number 0-913383 84 8
Library of Congress Card Catalog Number 2002102345

Cover design, cover photos and book layout by James Asher Graphics

Manufactured in the United States of America

All book order correspondence should be addressed to:
McClanahan Publishing House, Inc.
P. O. Box 100
Kuttawa, KY 42055

1-800-544-6959
www.kybooks.com
books@kybooks.com

Dedication

This book is dedicated to my beloved husband, Chuck Starr, for bringing so much love and light into my life. His being the most loving, encouraging, and supportive partner made this book possible. Thanks, Babe.

Tribute to my children

When I'm asked, "What is [illegible] greatest achievement?" I always answer, "My greatest achievement was having two terrific children." My son, Shane Highsmith, and my daughter, Ashley Highsmith, have always been the most loving, devoted, and inspiring children I could ever hope to have. This tribute extends to my daughter-in-law, Sarah, and my new grandson, Connor, who are a part of our circle of love that makes each of us truly blessed.

Table of Contents

Introduction

While I'm passing out my cards at club luncheons or other social events I hear some pretty entertaining remarks. People will ask, "Is this for real?" or say, "Wow, I've never met a real ghost hunter before." After a few minutes, I'll be surrounded by a small group anxious to tell me their very own experiences and seemingly happy to meet someone they can openly talk to about ghosts. These reactions validate my belief that our paradigm about the existence of ghosts and life after death is changing.

I grew up in the Piedmont area of South Carolina in a little town called Wellford. It was during that time I learned to love history. At fifteen, I moved with my family to Charleston, South Carolina. I was so intrigued by the history there and as most know, with history come the ghost stories.

Of course, over the years I rarely told anyone about my ghostly experiences. It wasn't until I moved to Kentucky that I started really searching for a way to research ghosts along with history. When I managed the Talbott Tavern, in Bardstown, I started getting unexplained mists, and orbs (globe-shaped lights), in the photos of planned events held there. With the advent of the computer and Internet I had a vehicle to lead me into areas that would reveal information about different anomalies involving paranormal activities that others were getting in their photos. I also became exposed to other ghost hunters who were seeing anomalies in their photos and getting moving anomalies in their videos and spirit voices on their audio recorders.

By 1996, this became more than a hobby. I began to document these experiences in a scientific manner. I [illegible]ed to be able [illegible]find a pattern or system that might add to the proof of life after death. I had no idea how many fields of knowledge would be opened to me. I found myself studying some of the works Einstein wrote about energy. I studied about solar weather and sun flares and how they affect the electro-magnetic fields of the earth, which might tie into a paranormal situation. I taught myself how to read different devices that measure these electro, microwaves, and magnetic fields during an investigation and what they meant. Soon I was buying books on human behavior, sleep disorders, and psychic talents. I developed an understanding of photography, and how audio recordings work with magnetic tapes that are used to capture the voices of the spirits. I began reading many topics and case studies on NDE (Near Death Experiences), and reviewed both sides of these as being spiritual experiences or as brain hormones being released at death, and began to draw my own conclusions.

I'm so grateful that I decided to learn about ghosts because it has led me into so many different avenues of life. I don't claim to know everything. As a matter of fact, the more I learn the more I realize how little I know, but I sure know a lot more today than I did before I started my research of ghosts and life after death.

I teach "Introductory to Ghost Hunting" at the Lexington Community College and it was so well received that I was asked to teach "Advanced Ghost Hunting," which includes three field trips of ghost investigations. I tell my students on their first day in class that ghost hunting is not an exact science. It is based on theory and conjecture that I have developed through my research and my own experiences. I ask them to have open minds and hold on to what makes sense to them and discard what they can't accept and have a little fun at learning something new.

I believe we are moving into a new area of spiritual awareness, where people are looking for answers. After reading this book, I feel confident that you will not only learn how to do an investigation of ghosts, but also learn how to go out and find them. My main objective is to change the fear that most people have about ghosts and replace it with understanding and compassion for these wandering souls.

Chapter 1

Who Can Be A Ghost Hunter?

*"While much is too strange to believe,
nothing is too strange to have happened."*
Thomas Hardy

Anyone can qualify to be a ghost hunter. Ghost hunting is a profession where most of the knowledge will be self taught and learned directly on the job. Knowledge is power and at the present time, most people have little if any knowledge about parapsychology. Most ghost hunters already believe in ghosts. It's the drive to understand the very nature and origin of the spirit world that leads people into the field. There have been great minds in all cultures and in all ages of time who have researched and written about the paranormal field.

Thomas Edison was one of these great minds who believed there was life after death. During Edison's lifetime, he invented the electric motor, phonograph, light bulb, typewriter, and over one thousand more patented inventions. One of his last inventions, a secret project, was a machine that would allow us to see and communicate with the dead. Edison referred to the soul as being made up of what he called, "life units." He found that these microscopic particles or life units could rearrange themselves into any form. They could retain their personalities and memory and were impossible to destroy. These life units would be detected in the environment through Edison's device and allow the living to communicate with the dead. Some scientists called him crazy, but others thought he was really on to something. Sadly, Edison died before he could finish his new creation. Can you imagine how different our world might be today if he had succeeded?

The toughest part of becoming a ghost hunter is learning how to go into an investigation thinking and acting like a skeptic. It's a duty to be open-minded and examine the facts for any logical explanations or possible frauds. Many investigators in the paranormal pursuit were once total disbelievers. Many set out to disprove claims made by psychics and other researchers. The evidence they uncovered was undeniable and so convincing that they became dedicated to sharing their insights with others.

Ghosts present science with a greater puzzle. They elude the reality of the real world. They play tricks on the human senses, confusing the mind with unexplained noises in the middle of the night, doors that lock from the inside when no one is in the room, strange smells, and cold spots. Science has no current way of examining or experimenting with ghosts. Therefore, when mainstream science cannot explain something it is immediately written off as unbelievable nonsense. Ghost hunters have studied and researched paranormal phenomena for decades and have been able to prove some clear-cut theories. It is true that not much is known about ghosts, but the work continues.

As of January 26, 2001, almost 70 million Americans believe it is possible to communicate with the dead and 42 percent of the population has even reported contact with the deceased, according to a CNN/USA Today/Gallup Poll and the National Research Council. However, most people are afraid to admit it for fear they will be labeled as kooky. Sometimes their own family will think they are delusional. Individuals who claim to see ghosts, communicate with spirits, hear voices, or have NDEs (Near Death Experiences) are diagnosed as mentally deranged and out of touch with reality. That's why it is so important for people who have seen ghosts or had paranormal experiences to know they are not alone. A ghost hunter will find there is no shortage of people with ghost stories to tell. Ghost stories have been told and retold since the dawn of history. Smart, well-educated people have reported strange supernatural phenomena. Whether scientists want to admit it or not, something is happening out there.

Physicist Befitting a Ghost Hunter

A dowsing rod held out in front of him, Stephen Marshall steps over the threshold and into Room 2 of the Old Stagecoach Inn. Almost immediately the device, which resembles a pair of rabbit ears, flips up and points toward the ceiling, even banging against his chest. Then as it straightens out he holds his dowser in front of him. "I'm hardly holding it. It should be falling on the floor," Marshall says. "This whole room is just loaded. Loaded with energy. Psychic energy, karmic energy, whatever you want to call it, ghost energy."

Stephen Marshall, a respected physicist who spent 27 years doing classified research on infrared technology and state-of-the-art weaponry for the Defense Department, is spending his retirement time tracking down ghosts. Marshall, who won't reveal his age and won't talk about his background, spent almost his entire professional career with the U.S. Army Corps of Engineers' Cold Regions Research and Engineering Laboratory in Hanover, N.H. What is his motive for ghost hunting?

"Scientific curiosity," he says. "It's a phenomenon nobody understands, so it interests me. And I want to see it documented scientifically, not haphazardly. Ghosts are a part of physics that hasn't been explored. It's the rest of the story."

One of the basic laws of physics is that energy can't be created or destroyed, but it can be transformed. Marshall says that ghosts have energy and are usually colder than their surroundings. He speculates that infrared technology, because it's sensitive to heat instead of light, might be useful in hunting ghosts. Marshall said he has always known he was a little psychic, although he never admitted it to his scientific colleagues for fear it would hurt his career. Even now, he's worried about becoming a laughingstock.

"Once you've done research all those years, you've got to

continue to research," Marshall says, "I always like to be first to discover whatever it is that I'm going to discover, whether it's good or not."

Becoming a Ghost Hunter

The ghost hunter goes into an investigation as a detective. This includes taking pictures, videos, audios, and registering equipment results. Being aware of all logical and natural explanations will aid in researching a reasonable conclusion.

A ghost hunter should treat each alleged haunted location like a crime scene. By meticulously going over the area and carefully gathering any physical evidence while not disturbing the area, one can analyze even the smallest clue left behind. It's always a plus to be able to refer to similar cases during the process of deduction. Once all the information is gathered you can defend your conclusion.

There is one important fact to remember when ghost hunting. There are no guarantees on predicting when or where a ghost will appear. So there won't be any rules or absolutes when ghost hunting. There are circumstances that seem to create more ghostly results, so we work with these. A ghost may appear once in a hundred years or every Tuesday. Some ghosts will haunt houses while others dwell in one small spot and others in an open field. Even if you have perfect conditions it doesn't mean a ghost will show up. When ghosts finally appear, even then they don't seem to follow a specific pattern. They make their presence known by sharp chills, balls of light, a peculiar odor, foggy mists, or apparitions of many shapes.

My goal as a ghost hunter is to find the most authentic evidence of the paranormal. I'm still making mistakes and just when I think I have some evidence that seems real I learn after putting my results through other tests that I was fooled. This is when I'm honest with myself, as well as others, and say, "Okay, I goofed. This is only a strand of my hair that got in the way of my video camera, which we originally thought to be orbs falling from the ceiling." Ouch! How embarrassing.

I want to make a concerted effort to show the best information and evidence that I can. I want to be better and not make foolish mistakes that may destroy the precious credibility I've worked so desperately to create. If I could send one very important message to all new ghost hunters, it is to always be careful with the evidence you collect. Do everything possible to make sure it is real before presenting it to the public. Your career as a ghost hunter will depend on this.

The best advice in becoming a ghost hunter is to research and learn all you can. Keep an open mind, but at the same time do your best to use logic to rule out those things that are explainable. Try to keep a balanced approach and have fun doing it. Remember, when it comes to ghost hunting, there is one rule—-be ready for anything!

In Spite of the fear, I Became a Ghost Hunter

The paranormal events that happened during my three years as general manager of the Talbott Tavern in Bardstown, KY, are some of the reasons why I got so interested in ghosts and then later became a Certified Ghost Hunter. Of course anyone who walks into this more than 200-year-old building can see how it could be haunted. The suggestion that ghosts are peering around a corner comes with an eerie feeling as you walk up the stairs to the guest rooms, glancing behind you as the hair rises on the back of your neck. The tavern has had many owners and visitors who stayed and died there. Just across the back alley is the Jailer's Inn, which was the county jail from 1800 to 1985, where many men were hung for their crimes. So, with all this in mind, it's easy to understand why the spirits were waiting in the wings and roaming the corridors of the tavern.

My first experience came when I had to open early one January morning. It was a cold, gray day and with no sun it was very dark as I entered the building. I wasn't scared at first. I started turning on lights and closing out registers to start the day's business. Then it was time to take the reports upstairs to my office and get the register cash drawers. As I started up the dark stairs about halfway up I felt a rush of cold air, as though a draft were present. As I felt it an incredible fear swept over me as well. I stopped and looked up into the dark and tried to go forward but could not make my feet move. It became

Mysterious mist in dining room at the Talbott Tavern, in Bardstown, Kentucky with a slight form of a child sitting in the chandelier. Mike McGrath took this picture on Halloween night in 1997.

very hard for me to catch my breath and my breathing became very labored. I decided to go back down the stairs when my feet were able to move again.

When I got to the bottom of the stairs I looked back up and felt very threatened and terrified. I tried telling myself that I was being silly and to just go on up the stairs. I was on a time schedule and had to get the reports done and the money in the registers before the employees started coming in to work. I decided to walk around and check out the dining rooms and kitchen, thinking that would help calm me and at least slow down my heart rate. Everything else in the building was fine and the fear inside me slowly subsided.

Now that the fear was gone I picked up my register reports and started back up the steps. About halfway up the same thing happened and I was frozen in place with this unnerving fear and struggled to catch my breath. I turned and went back down the stairs and thought about what to do next. I told myself I was being silly and that I had to go to my office or I was going to cause the whole oper-

In the lower right corner of the photo, notice the round ball shaped (orbs) anomalies in a moving motion. This photo was taken in the Jesse James room at Talbott Tavern. Unfortunately, the fire destroyed most of this room in 1998 but you can still see the alleged bullet holes that were made by Jesse James as the legend goes.

ation to be late in getting started. This time I made up my mind, no matter what, I would make it to the top of the stairs.

I went up the stairs again and didn't stop this time. The cold spot and the fear hit me about halfway up just as before but this time I made it to the top. It was so dark I had to run my hands along the wall to find the light switch. My heart was about to pound out of my chest. My knees were buckling under me and I could hardly walk. I just knew that as soon as I turned on the light a horrible distorted creature from hell would be glaring down at me. Of course, that was not the case and I was so relieved to get the light on.

I had to go down another hall to turn on the rest of the lights and because I had some light I was able to see where I was going. The presence was still with me and I was still shaking in my shoes while looking behind me with every step I took. As I got closer to the other light switch it became darker and darker and more difficult for me to see where the switch was. At this point my mind was racing with thoughts of old horror flicks where the heroine goes down that dark hallway and everyone in the audience is yelling for her not to go. When I made it to the other light switch, I reached out to turn on the lights and just at that second I screamed out a sound I never knew I possessed. The furniture in the opposite room started to vibrate heavily across the floor. I thought a train was traveling towards me. I turned quickly back to the light switch and turned on the lights. In that instant the sound stopped. I stared into the room, where the light from the hallway slanted in through the door, expecting to see a twisted mess of furniture. To my surprise, everything was in place without any signs of movement. At this point I just turned and ran to the other side of the building, where my office was, to get away from whatever had been in that room.

When I reached my office door, as in most horror flicks, I was fumbling through my hundreds of keys to find the one that opened the door. I felt something was coming toward me and any minute would round the corner and take me. I was shaking so hard that when I finally found the key and tried to put it in the keyhole I dropped my keys on the floor. Now I thought, I'm certain I'm a goner, but I continued to scramble for my keys and tried again to unlock the door. When I finally made it into my office I slammed my door and backed up until I hit my desk and could go no farther.

I took some deep breaths and turned my back to the door to hang up my coat. Just as I did something very heavy hit the door. It hit so hard I could feel the vibration of the blow all the way across the room. I swung around and without any thought of what I was doing ran over to the door as fast as I could and locked the deadbolt. Then I ran back to the other end of the room. By now I was crying and really afraid that maybe someone was in the building with intent to hurt me.

I put my hand on the phone to call 911 but stopped. I thought about how silly I would sound when I told them about what happened. I'd be laughed at as the spooked blond who let her imagination get the best of her. I was already late and the first employee was scheduled to arrive any minute and I had nothing ready. I decid-

Notice the ectoplasmic mist coming up from the floor. Patti Starr took this photo at the Talbott Tavern in the basement in 1998.

ed I would wait a little longer to see if anything else happened before I called the police. I sat down to relax and gather my senses in order to leave my office to get the money from the safe. By this time it was 8 o'clock and the streets were getting busy with traffic. I knew I had to go down and let my secretary in, so I couldn't just sit there.

I finally got the nerve to unlock and open my office door. I slowly stuck my head out and looked up the north hall and then the west hall and everything felt fine. As I walked out into the hall toward the steps I was very apprehensive, but the feeling I had before was totally gone. I felt calm, my breathing was normal, and I wondering to myself, "How in the world did I let my imagination get the best of me." I walked on down the hall and opened the door to the room where I felt the furniture move. It was still very dark, so I hesitated to reach in around the corner to turn on the lights. But I chuckled to myself and remembered an old horror flick in which the actor puts his hand through a door opening to turn on the light and whack, off went his hand. But getting over that I turned on the light and everything was fine. Nothing was out of order and I began to realize that I had not imagined all of what had happened to me.

I turned out the light and went down the hall toward the safe room, as we called it, to get the money out of the safe. When I unlocked that door to go in I again felt a big drop in the temperature and thought to myself, "Oh, no not again." I did feel a presence in the room with me, but this time it was different. It was not the same feeling I had by the stairs, but it was still spooky. It was calmer and it almost felt as though a female was reassuring me that everything was going to be all right.

I took the money from the safe, looking over my shoulder several times, expecting to see a ghostly figure of a woman hovering over me. That never happened, or at least that's not what I saw, but felt.

I managed to make it back to my office and started my reports for the day's business. I let the employees in downstairs, but didn't tell anyone what had just happened to me. I was afraid if I started to talk about it I would not be able to come back in the morning, and since this was the job I loved, I didn't want to hurt my career. So I decided to deal with whatever was there at the tavern and to make the best of the situation. Boy, was I in for some more surprises!

Chapter 2

Ghosts & Spiritualism

"Is death the last step?
No, it is the final awakening."
Sir Walter Scott

From the ancient past to the present day, communication between the Earth Plane and the Spirit World has been a factor in the lives of individuals. People from every country in the world have been able to communicate with ghosts or spirits. Some religions have had the idea of spiritual communication as their foundations. During the era of Christianity, the Apostle Paul taught that there is a spiritual body and a physical body. While on earth, the body takes on successive bodies until it perfects its course. The spiritual body dwells in the Heavenly Realm and a place is reserved for this body by God. Through this teaching, Paul brought forth another foundation for the understanding of immortality. Here we see this spiritual communication foundation built into Christianity through the mediumistic ability the disciples confirmed. Also, in the Christian era, belief in the supernatural power was accepted. As years went by, the priesthood became the controlling force and only they were permitted to heal the sick, predict the future, and master the art of divining, as in dowsing.

In changing with the times during the Dark Ages, dealing in

healings, spells, fortune telling, or anything known as witchcraft or sorcery, was proclaimed as illegal. Then as the years slipped into the Middle Ages, the practice of witchcraft was tainted by the church's belief it was in league with the Devil. Before this definition of witchcraft came about, it was simply known as sorcery and magic at work. Coming into the Witchcraft Era from the 15th century through the 18th century, priests were no longer permitted to predict the future, heal the sick or communicate with spirit entities. By doing so anyone could easily be branded as a witch consorting with the devil.

History of Modern Spiritualism

On March 31, 1848, in the small village of Hayesville, N.Y., two young girls, Margarita Fox, age fourteen, and Catherine Fox, age twelve, unknowingly were the major participants in the Spiritual Movement. On this evening, as the family was preparing to go to bed after a very exhausting day, the phenomena began. The same tapping noise they had been hearing for the last few months had started up again in one of the bedrooms. During the past winter months all sorts of unexplained disturbances had been noted. Tapping that became stronger and stronger continued and then additional phenomena took place. Furniture was moved, footsteps in the hallway and down the stairs to the cellar could be heard, and touches by an unseen hand were experienced. Mrs. Fox was convinced the place was haunted.

One of the little girls, Catherine, decided to clap her hands to see if the entity could mimic her claps and to everyone's amazement the same number of taps were returned. Mrs. Fox decided to ask questions and discovered that if the answer was no, there would be no reply, but if the answer was yes, there would be two taps. Through yes-and-no questions Mrs. Fox was able to affirm that there was a male entity who had been murdered in the house and whose body was buried in the cellar. He claimed to have been a 31-year-old father of five children. He had been killed for $500.

The next day the Fox family decided to start digging in the cellar. Because it was the rainy season of March, they hit water within a few feet, so the digging was postponed to a later date. After a while, the water subsided and in July they started to dig again. This time they found traces of charcoal, pieces of pottery, and something that looked like human hair and pieces of bone. Later, they learned from a medical examiner that the hair was of human origin and the pieces of bone were part of a human skull.

During a short period between 1842 and 1843, this same cottage housed the Bell family, which had a live-in housekeeper, Lucreta Pulver. One day a well-known peddler came calling on Mrs. Bell and Lucreta joined the gathering in the parlor. While the ladies were looking over the wares, Lucreta picked out some fine material she wanted to buy for a dress. Before she could finish her transaction, Mrs. Bell left the room and called Lucreta out into the kitchen. Mrs. Bell dismissed Lucreta, telling her that her services were no longer needed and that she should leave. Shocked at the sudden dismissal, Lucreta gathered her belongings and asked the peddler to deliver her material to her home the next day.

For some strange reason, the peddler never showed up at Lucreta's home, but three days later Mrs. Bell did. She hired Lucreta back into service, so they returned to the cottage. Mrs. Bell expressed her gratitude to Lucreta for returning by giving her some of the gifts and keepsakes she had bought from the peddler.

Soon after Lucreta settled back into her room at the cottage, she began to witness eerie happenings. She was awakened in the night by tapping at the foot of her bed. When she complained to Mrs. Bell about the noise and her fear, Mrs. Bell assured her she was just dreaming. As this continued to wake her in the night, Lucreta realized what was happening to her was not a dream, but very real. Soon the tapping increased all over the house and the Bells blamed the sounds on rats. One afternoon, Lucreta went to the cellar for kitchen supplies and before returning stepped into an area of soft dirt and sank down so deep she had to scream for help. After being pulled out of the dirt, Lucreta was told by the Bells that rats had been digging in the cellar floor, which was why that area was so soft she sank. Mr. Bell immediately had the cellar floor filled with more dirt he packed down to make the floor more stable. As the disturbances continued, Lucreta decided it was too nerve wracking for her and she moved back home to her mother's place. Mr. and Mrs. Bell moved out of the cottage in 1843 and were never heard of again.

After the Fox family moved out of the cottage, the girls continued receiving messages from the spirit world. They claimed to be instructed by the spirits to go out and let people know that it was possible to communicate with spirits. The girls demonstrated their ability to speak to the spirits and get a response by table tapping. Some observers watched in amazement while others became suspicious of this talent and presumed the girls were fakes. These trials and tribulations continued all through their lives. Both sisters' psychic talents fell in and out of favor with the public until their lives ended in the 1890's, due largely to alcoholism. Despite all the problems they faced and endured, Modern Spiritualism came about as a result of their talented lives.

On November 23, 1904, fifty-six years after the tapping in the cottage was first recorded, this report was printed in *The Boston Journal:*

The skeleton of the man supposed to have caused the rappings first heard by the Fox sisters in 1848 has been found in the walls of the house occupied by the sisters, and clears them from the only shadow of doubt, held concerning their sincerity in the discovery of spirit communications.

The Fox sisters declared they learned to communicate with the spirit of a man and that he told them he had been murdered and buried in the cellar. Repeated excavations failed to locate the body and this gives proof positive of their story.

The discovery was made by school children playing in the cellar of the building in Hydesville, known as the "spook house," where the Fox sisters heard the wonderful rappings. William H. Hyde, a reputable citizen of Clyde, who owns the house, made an investigation and found an almost entire human skeleton between the earth and crumbling cellar walls, undoubtedly that of a wandering peddler who, is claimed to have been murdered in the east room of the house, and whose body was hidden in the cellar.

Mr. Hyde notified relatives of the Fox sisters, and the notice of discovery will be sent to the National Order of Spiritualists, many

of whom remember having made pilgrimages to the "spook house," as it is commonly called. The findings of the bones practically corroborates the sworn statement made by Margaret Fox, April 11, 1848. The Fox sisters claimed to have been disturbed by the rappings and finally by a system of signals got into communication with the spirit.

According to Margaret Fox's statement, the Spirit was that of a peddler, who described how he had been murdered in the house, his body being buried in the cellar. There were numerous witnesses to the rappings, but although the cellar had been dug up many times, no traces of the body had been found until the crumbling cellar walls revealed the skeleton.

The name of the murdered man according to his revelation to the Fox sisters, was Charles Rosna, and the murderer, a man named Bell. In 1847, the house was occupied by Michael Weekman, a poor laborer. He and his family became troubled by the mysterious rappings, which followed in succession at different intervals, especially during the night. The family became so broken by fear and loss of sleep that they vacated the house. On December 11, 1847 The Fox family moved in and two months later the rappings were resumed and the family frightened. Finally, Margaretta and Cathie grew bold and asked questions which were answered, revealing the murder.

Journal Editor's note: Attention is drawn to the fact that a portion of the skull (which the foregoing report declares to be missing) was discovered during the digging operations at the time of the "knockings"-1848.

My Ghost Revealed

All I could do was toss and turn as I tried to go to sleep that night. Many worries filled my head and kept me from finding that peaceful place to forget my undecided future. My daddy lay in a nearby hospital with no hopes of recovery and the doctor sent me home to get some rest. He told me to try and get some sleep since I had been awake for two days after my 18-hour flight from Europe. So I went to my mom's place, fell into the sleeper and finally started to drift off as I gave way to my exhaustion, and fell into a deep sleep.

The doctor had warned our family that my dad may have only a few more hours of life, so many of our out-of-town relatives had come to Mom's house to stay the night. She had given up her bed to my aunt and uncle while she and I slept on the living room sofa bed. During my deep sleep I woke up suddenly with the strange feeling someone was in the room and watching me. I felt a very frightening presence and knew I had to roll over and look around the room. It was very dark, with only a street light shining through the main window so it took a while to search the room. It was August and the room was too cold for that time of year. There was also a strange odor that I couldn't identify. By this time I knew what was going to happen. This was not the first time I had awakened to this type of experience. I pulled the covers closer to my face and peered out into the dark room. All of a sudden, as if growing from the ground, stood the figure of a very big man. I couldn't see his face, but his outline was so threatening I just sat up in bed and started to scream at the top of my lungs. My mother, sleeping beside me, woke up and also sat up screaming.

My aunt and uncle came running into the living room to see what was going on. Uncle Bob turned on the light and he saw us staring ahead screaming. As the light flashed on and brightened the room, we stopped screaming and turned to each other with startled stares. No one said a word. I looked around the room but nothing seemed to be out of place. Of course, there was no sign of the tall, dark stranger.

I was so embarrassed by what had just happened that I apologized to everyone and told them to go back to bed because it was just a bad dream. I knew Uncle Bob would get a big laugh if I told him that I had seen a spirit or ghost. I knew my mom would only say I had a bad dream and try to convince me that what I saw wasn't real, but the result of the stress I was feeling over Dad's condition. This is how she handled it when I was a little girl.

This same man often visited me during my entire childhood. He came into my room and quietly watched me sleep until the cold

This is a misty anomaly with round ball shapes (orbs) moving in the mist over my son's head. This is the same room where mom and I witnessed the man standing over us when we woke up. This photo was taken in mom's home in Charleston, South Carolina, in 1970 by Eunice Nabors.

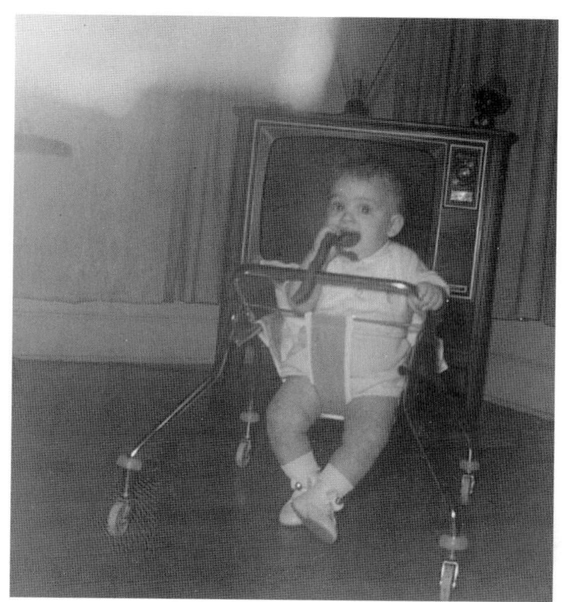

and smell woke me up. Then I watched him walk around looking at my things. Sometimes he picked up my clothes or toys and looked at me to dare me to move. Many times I wanted to scream for my parents but his threatening looks kept me silent until he started to approach my bed. Then I knew I had to start screaming or something terrible was going to happen. Sometimes I watched him run out of the room before my mom or dad could get to me. Other times he charged at me and I covered my head and screamed until my parents came to my rescue. Sometimes they tried to pull the cover off my face so they could calm me down, but I was convinced it was this spirit or ghost trying to get to me first.

About two years after my dad's illness, from which he did recover, I was visiting with my mom at a family gathering. We were all sitting around talking and laughing about funny events that had happened to us over the years. My uncle, laughing, talked about how we scared the daylights out of him the night he woke up to hear me and my mom screaming at the tops of our lungs in the living room. I told them the reason I was screaming was that I had seen a huge black figure of a man standing at the foot of our sleeper, glaring down at us.

In the top right corner is a bright white anomaly that appears in the same room where my mom and I saw the figure of a man standing over us. This photo was taken in my mom's home in Charleston, South Carolina, 1973 by Wanda Belcher.

At that moment my mother grabbed my arm and said, "That is exactly why I was screaming. I saw the same man." For a moment there was only silence. This was the first time my mom had ever admitted to me that I had seen something, without her insisting that I was dreaming or that it was my imagination. I said to her, "You see Mom, this is what used to scare me in my room when I was a little girl and I'm glad that you finally got to see it." After that, Mom didn't hesitate to listen to me when I had a ghostly experience to share with her.

Years later, after I had studied and researched ghosts and learned how to capture them on film, I decided to go back and see if I could find any pictures of this house that might have locked in on a ghost or spirit. To my delight, I found three pictures that revealed definite anomalies, similar to the ones I get in the photos of my research in today's hauntings.

I called my sister, Wanda Belcher, to see if she had had any weird experiences happen in that same house. To my joy, she did have a story to share with me. She said that one night she woke up to the sound of Grandpa's jew's-harp playing. A few years after our grandpa died, my mom decided to give Wanda his favorite musical instruments, two jew's-harps. Mom gave them to her wrapped up in a hanky inside a small box. My sister wanted to keep them forever because she was so fond of our grandpa, so she put the box in her cedar chest. That night she was awakened by the sound of a jew's-harp playing. At first she thought she was sleeping but the longer she lay there the more it became clear to her that it was the sound of the jew's-harp she had heard Grandpa play many times before his passing. It was a sound that brought back sweet memories of Grandpa playing happy tunes as she danced about with him. She became frightened and covered her head with the pillow, so she couldn't hear it any more and finally fell back to sleep.

The next morning after being up for a while she remembered her dream. She decided to check to see if the jew's-harps were still in her cedar chest. When she opened her chest, there on the first shelf was the open box and the jew's-harps, lying to the side, unwrapped from the hanky. She was too scared to tell anyone what had happened so she just wrapped them up and put them back into the chest. I think most of us are afraid to tell these stories of unexplained experiences for fear others will think we are crazy or somehow unstable. I'm so glad she decided to share her story with me. It just helps to know that I was not the only one in that house who had lived through a ghostly experience.

Chapter 3

The Different Types of Hauntings

"Nothing in life is to be feared. It is only to be understood."

Marie Curie

While we try to organize and categorize ghosts and hauntings, many spirits and other phenomena tend to disregard all rules. Certain paranormal activity just doesn't fit into any classification. We still have to make an attempt to group these different ghosts and hauntings into categories so we will know how to handle situations.

You might say that all genuine paranormal phenomena, which we have been trained to ignore, continue to press into our consciousness. These meta-phenomena are slowly revealing another side to our existence. While we may not know the mechanism involved, we continue to look for ways to make the paranormal clearer to us. In summary, I have categorized a few of the most common types of ghosts and hauntings, as we know them.

Intelligent Hauntings

The intelligent haunting is probably the most traditional of all. Spirits or ghosts involved with the haunting are there because of a connection to the site or the people. The site could be their residence before they died. Or while wandering after their death, they find a place that reminds them of a happy time in their former life and decided to stay there. If it's people who have drawn them to the site, it could be a grieving loved one for whom they feel an attachment, or after their death they start looking for a family similar to the one they had while still alive on earth. These ghosts have personalities, emotions, reasoning, and other human traits, just as they had before they passed on. Some do not realize they are dead. This could be due to the way they died. If their deaths were quick and unexpected, they may still be trying to figure out what happened to them. Other factors may be involved, as well. These ghosts may have unfinished business to handle. If they feel guilty about a sin or action they committed while living, they may fear being judged or even punished if they proceed to the other side. Also, many times a loved one will grieve so strongly that the ghost stays behind for fear of leaving them too soon.

One thing I would like to clear up is referring to ghosts as being evil or demonic. People often ask me if I get scared when I go on a ghost hunt. I tell them honestly that it is very seldom that I'm afraid. When I go into a haunted building or site, I know that most likely the spirit there will be more of a reflection of me and the people in my environment. It would only make sense for this to be true. These ghosts maintain the same personalities, desires, fears, and knowledge they had in life, so why not carry these traits over into death? Are you afraid of any of the people in your life and environment? How many people do you know who are truly evil? Probably none. You may know a mean person or an angry person or even a bitter person, but that doesn't make any of these persons evil. The same is true of ghosts. Most of them are of the same nature as you and me.

Now that is not to say that there are not ghosts with negative personalities. They exist just as some of the people in our lives have negative personalities. These ghosts may have lived lives filled with anger, or hate for everything, or bitterness towards others, so it would be natural for them to carry this sort of personality with them to the other side. If I do run into a nasty ghost, I try to find out who or what makes them mean or violent and try to make contact with them, so they can continue to the other side.

Residual Hauntings

This type of haunting can easily be confused with intelligent hauntings because of their similarities. Even though you still have sounds, voices, or see images, the spirit is not present. There are two common assumptions about residual hauntings.

To start with, there could have been a tragic event so strong that it leaves an imprint (sometimes referred to as psychic impressions) in the locale of the tragedy. At certain intervals of time, the residual haunting will replay the event with sights and sounds that have no explanation. The horrific event could be a group of participants fighting and dying in a battle or a bus full of people crashing off a bridge and drowning. Instead of a haunting on the battlefield or the bridge, you have a residual haunting caused by an imprint of an event replaying the story.

When someone claims to hear footsteps, especially if they hear them at a certain time and in a particular place, this is more likely a residual haunting, instead of a ghost. Most imprints are created by the event being repeated over and over. That's why so many people report hearing footsteps on the stairs or down hallways. Walking up and down stairs and hallways over time may cause imprints. If one worked in an area for several years and had to perform a certain job, in a certain way, in a certain place, over and over again, in time this person or persons could make an imprint in that locale. Over time this former action could start replaying the imprint and likely create a residual haunting.

Sometimes when I hear a report of an apparition being seen in period clothing I think of this as an image of time being an imprint on the location. Apparitions that are usually seen in the same areas, performing the same tasks without noticing others around them are usually good examples of residual hauntings.

One important thing to mention is that unlike dealing with a ghost, when you are involved with a residual haunting, items will not disappear and then reappear in different places.

Poltergeist Activity

A poltergeist is a noisy and sometimes violent ghost. The name "poltergeist" has Greek roots meaning "noisy ghost." Known actions of the poltergeist are banging, thumping, moving objects, levitating, and causing fires. These same happenings can also be the result of an unconscious outburst of psychokinesis.

Poltergeist activity is the most misdiagnosed of all hauntings. At one time it was thought that the paranormal forces were coming from an angry ghost or demonic entity. These cases were reported to have a variety of phenomena connected to them. There would be knocking on doors and walls, lights going off and on, televisions and appliances going off and on, furnishings being moved, fires breaking out, and objects flying through the air.

Poltergeist records have gone back as far as medieval days in China and Germany. The records show unexplainable events such as flying objects, loud noises, dirt throwing, terrible smells, apparitions, and bright lights. These incidents have been known to last for a few hours or a few years. The difference between poltergeist activity and a haunting can be very hard to distinguish. A ghost that seems to appear frequently in certain places at certain times by moving objects, slamming doors, or turning lights on and off, could be classified as a haunting. Then again these same occurrences could be attributed to a form of psychokinetic energy coming unknowingly from a living person. Paranormal activities that remain constant over time in a general area could be considered a haunting. When you have paranormal activities that continue to increase to a climax and then calm down again only to start the cycle over are usually considered to be those of a poltergeist. The paranormal events of a haunting are not usually of a violent nature, whereas the poltergeist can become dangerous and may cause physical or mental harm.

More and more researchers are now convinced that most of these outbreaks are not results of an angry ghost or demonic entity, but the unconscious discharge of psychokinesis (the ability to move objects with the mind). The person responsible for this action is usually a young female under twenty years of age and suffering from psychological stress. It is also possible for this phenomenon to happen to young males or adults, but by the largest accounts, it happens to young females most often.

Sometimes these harsh activities can be the result of a very emotional intelligent spirit trying to get someone to notice them. Once you have eliminated the psychokinetic theory, you can conclude that the haunting is a poltergeist in its original form.

Crisis Apparitions

These apparitions appear to family and friends at the moment the crisis occurs or just at death. The crisis ghost appears one last time to say a final goodbye, fulfill a promise, or to express its love to help ease the sadness of death for the individual left behind. The apparition is believed to have a strong telepathic connection between the person and witness.

Family Apparitions

Some ghosts may attach themselves to particular families. They tend to haunt each member of a family throughout the generations. The appearance of these ghosts sometimes means that a family member is going to die soon. This person could become suddenly ill and die or be terminally injured, causing an untimely death. Once the family member has figured out what is meant by the ghost's presence, he or she may make attempts to get rid of it. No matter what they try — spells, exorcisms, or prayers — the apparition will not leave. Some believe that the ghost is a demon and causing the deaths, while others see it as a warning of what is in store for the family member. Usually this type of haunting will stop only when the family line comes to an end.

Haunted Articles

A ghost can become very attached to an article. It could be a piece of furniture, a lamp, book, figurine, clock, plant, or a piece of clothing, with which the past owner had a very emotional tie when he was alive. After death, he remains very much attached to the item. These objects can be present during strange occurrences, which might include sounds and lights coming from the area where these objects are found. They might be seen moving or vibrating on their own. Sometimes a shadow will be seen near the article.

Portal Hauntings

Based strictly on theory, some ghost researchers think that a "portal" (doorway) exists to another dimension. These openings exist all over the world and serve as doorways that provide access for the entities to enter this world. As these portals are discovered, the spirits are there because they provide them with a means of passing in and out of our world. They are not there because of a tragic event or any reason other than travel. These ghostly gateways are like the hypothetical worm holes believed by some cosmologists to link different universes. So what could be considered haunted may be just a kind of spectral turnstile to and from the other side.

Can ghosts hurt us? I don't think so, at least not the discarnate personalities of the dead. There are cases of people being bitten, scratched, or pushed down in hauntings, but most of these were found to be caused by human agents and not ghosts. In some other cases where a strange creature is described as grotesque, being injured by this terrifying entity is another mystery. What if these creatures are not ghosts, but strange entities that we just don't understand? Maybe they have come into our world through these portals.

Usually these portal hauntings occur in places where people report seeing glowing balls of light, odd creatures, strange shapes, or misty fog. A lot of these types of sightings happen at cemeteries. Why so many cemeteries over other places? These sites were probably haunted before the cemeteries were placed there. Maybe the person who chose the spot for the cemetery was drawn there because it made them feel there was something hallowed or sacred about the area, not knowing it was a portal haunting. The American Indian always searched for sacred grounds to bury their dead. How did they determine it was sacred ground? Was it a feeling? Did they notice a strange misty fog at times in that same area? Who knows?

Going to the Witches' Cemetery

It was late afternoon by the time my husband Chuck, and I went to the "Witches' Cemetery" with Jason Lewis, his wife Susan, magazine writer for *Today's Woman*, Mary Jo Harrod and her sister Jennifer Wright. I had previously checked out this cemetery for my students to do a ghost investigation for a class credit. James White, a psychic I met a few weeks prior at a local psychic fair, met me at the cemetery to lead me around and tell me its history. He explained how this spot was awarded the name "Witches' Cemetery." It was rumored that members of a cult of Wicca used the cemetery to conduct certain rituals and perform sessions of meditation. Since the area of this small "city of the dead" was so energized, the participants claimed to be able to perform their objectives more completely here during their ceremonies. He also told us how back in the fifties and sixties they buried homeless people in this same area.

Before the six of us entered this small, concealed burial ground, I recapped to my group what James told Chuck and me about the "Keeper" of the cemetery and that we were to enter only with the spirit's permission. He told us to stand behind him and wait as we watched for a sign for the keeper's consent to be granted. James explained that it could be a touch on the cheek or a warm feeling of welcome granting us permission. I demonstrated to everyone how James instructed us to enter through the opening and walk towards the center. As we continued forward, I stopped everyone from going to the center, just as James stopped me on our first visit. He instructed us to walk the parameters first until the spirits got used to our being there. He told us that the center was reserved for the "Keeper."

Knowing that this was a new experience for some of the people who were with me, I had them follow the same instructions.

As the writer and my group were walking around, I remembered how I felt the first time I visited this place. I'm not a psychic, but I am very sensitive to certain energies, so it didn't take long for me to pick up some very strong vibrations. As a result, I became a little light-headed. It was almost euphoric. As I looked around, I could see waves of energy coming up from the ground, as if one was looking at a road on a very hot day and could see the heat waves searing off the road, distorting the view ahead. Since I was teaching a course in advanced ghost hunting at the Lexington Community College, one of our field trips requires us to go to a cemetery. I knew almost immediately this was going to be a great place to bring my students for a ghost hunt.

I told Mary Jo about the pinch on my leg during my first visit there. James had called my attention to a very old oak tree and I was looking up into its gigantic arms when suddenly I yelped out in pain and jumped a couple of feet ahead as something bit the back of my leg. I turned around to see if I had stepped on a twig that had flipped up and hit me, or if I had backed into a tree stump that pierced the back of my leg, but there was nothing in sight. I bent over to rub the sting from the pain and James said it was one of the lady ghosts trying to get my attention. I thought, "Well, she got it alright." This was the first time I had been attacked by a ghost or spirit, so I thought. Later I found out that it was not a negative act but merely a way of trying to get my attention. The next day when I checked the back of my leg to see if I had any kind of teeth marks, I noticed that the bruise was horizontal. Then I figured it must have been more of a hard pinch than a bite.

After this little pinching episode, I immediately ran to the car and got my mini-cassette recorder, hoping I might get lucky and have some of the spirits speak to me. I got three voices, but the best one was a comment made by a ghost as I was showing my husband a leaf that had been infected with some sort of fungus. I lifted the leaf in my hand and said, "Look, Honey, there is some kind of fungus all over this leaf," and the ghost's voice said, "Ah, how terrible."

My husband came around behind me and took some pictures of the headstones and the surrounding stone fence. We had the film developed and noticed an anomaly in one of the photos next to the headstone. It looked like a spectra coffin coming up through the ground. It was a rosy, purple color outlined in a thin blue line. I took the photo to a professional photography studio where Tony Seelbach checked it for possibilities of damaged film, faulty processing, or light leaking into the camera. After careful examination he reported that it was an unexplained anomaly.

After explaining all the first-time experiences in the cemetery to Mary Jo for her article, we continued to canvass the place, taking a few snapshots with our cameras. Jason was very interested in the dowsing I perform as part of my method of getting information during a ghost investigation. By asking "yes and no" questions, I can find out if the ghosts are males or females, if they were married, had children, how old they were when they died, and what year they died. Then we can take the information and look up the history of the location and usually find out if there was someone who had lived there with the same description. Jason wanted me to show him how I used the two brass rods as I looked for the hot spots where the ghosts would be found. After demonstrating this technique, the mosquitoes were getting the best of us, so we thought we would call it quits. It was getting pretty dark and we didn't want to start falling over the broken headstones that were barely protruding from the ground.

We backed out of the cemetery as a gesture of respect and we gave thanks for the visit and for the ghosts' kindness to us. As I looked out across the darkness, I could see a mist rising from the ground. Then I realized I was actually seeing what we refer to as ecto-plasmic mist. I said, "Oh, my goodness!" And Jason, a psychic, said, "What? Do you see the mist, too?" I responded, "Yes, I do!" We asked the others if they could see the mist, but no matter how hard they looked they could not see the mist we saw. This was not a mist that was created by weather conditions or everyone would have been able to see it. I was pleasantly surprised when I got my film developed and found in two of the photos we had captured the mist that looked exactly like what Jason and I had seen.

Gathering around a picnic bench just outside the cemetery plot, we began to recap some of the things we had witnessed and felt. Jason decided to go back over to the stone fence that surrounded the small plot and see if he could pick up anything that would help identify why this place seemed to be so haunted. After a few minutes, I decided to join him to see if I had any more luck with my senses, as well. Being the complete writer that Mary Jo was, she decided to join us. I asked Jason what he could see or feel. He began to tell me that he had sensed a male presence and then he pointed to a figure that he saw through the trees that was looking back at him. No matter how hard I tried, I just couldn't see what he was describing. Looking straight ahead, I noticed something in the corner of my eye move and it startled me just a little, so I turned to see what the movement was. I could see a misty, gray form of a lady kneeling down with her head on the stone fence, crying. She was so sad and I could feel her pain. I asked Jason to look to the same area but he could not see what I was talking about. After a few moments, she slowly faded away and then I stepped into the area thinking I would feel a cold spot. Instead, it was very warm. When Jason came over, we both stretched out our hands and could feel the heat. Mary Jo said, "Don't you think the heat might be coming off the stones, since it was a pretty warm day today?" But when we laid our hands on the stone they were not hot at all, so the heat was not coming from the stones.

Being anxious to share this information with our group, we returned to the picnic table. While we were there, my friend James came by and was surprised to see me again so soon after our first meeting there at the cemetery. I explained I was showing the area to a writer who was doing an article on ghost hunting. After the introductions, he decided to go down to the little cemetery and sit for a while. He said he likes the energy and it helps him meditate. We were about to finish up our visit since Mary Jo and Jennifer had a two-hour drive ahead of them and it was already after ten o'clock. James came back to join us to say goodbye, and just out of curiosity, I asked him if he had seen anything while he was in the cemetery. I was amazed at what he began to describe to us.

"First thing I noticed when I entered the grounds was a thick mist about knee high. Then within a few minutes I observed a male spirit standing between two trees on the other side of the plot, just outside the wall. Later I noticed there was a woman and she was very sad as she sat on the ground just outside the stonewall fence," James explained as we listened in amazement. James had just described every event that Jason and I experienced only minutes earlier.

When I got home I was pretty anxious to listen to my mini recorder to see if I had gotten any ghost voices that we refer to as EVPs (Electronic Voice Phenomenon). I was thrilled that I did pick up a very strange sound this time. It was a sound that reminded me of an old fifties movie as you watched the UFO spacecraft hover over the ground. I sent it to a couple of electronic engineers and they had no explanation for me, so I figured I had a pretty convincing sound anomaly. I gave great thought to the possibility of a portal of some type being in this cemetery, with all the activity that we were able to measure.

The next Wednesday when I met with my class, I was very anxious to report to the students about the wonderful results we recorded in just a twenty-minute investigation when we met with James. Usually, to get any good results on an investigation you need to have two to four hours of collecting data from the various devices and equipment. After sharing my photos showing the coffin-shape anomaly and the EVPs of a male voice saying, "Ah, so terrible," all the students were really looking forward to going on this investigation.

Case Study Report of The Witches' Cemetery

In teaching this advanced course of ghost hunting, I require students to write complete reports of their findings in a scientific manner after they complete field ghost investigations. I have included the report from the Witches' Cemetery to show how and in what order we collect information.

Ghost Chaser International
Case Study Report of Paranormal Activity

Case #: 115

Description of Location: Witches' Cemetery

Date: August 22, 2001 Day: Wednesday__

Time In: 6:30 p.m. **Time Out:** 8:30 p.m.

Weather: Sunny Temp.: H 87/ L 70
Humidity: 75%
Barometric: 30.13 & falling
Solar Rays: M-Class Flare
Geomagnetic Field: Unsettled
Lunar Phase: 3 days after the New Moon

Investigators Present:

1) Patti Starr
2) Chuck Starr
3) Paula Lewis
4) Kristen Myers
5) Pat Crowe
6) Tom Zumwalt
7) Susan Rummel

8) Lori Baker
9) Bill Bailey
10) Daelen Richardson
11) Mike Clark
12) Tory Eldridge
13) Brice Foster

Spectators Present:

1) Mary Jo Harrod
2) Jennifer Wright

List of Equipment & Devices:

1) 35 mm cameras
2) Nikon 950 digital camera
3) Mini cassette audio recorder
4) Regular tape audio recorder
5) Sony Night Shot camcorder
6) Gauss EMF meter
7) TriField Natural EM meter
8) Laser beam light
9) Compass
10) Brass dowsing rods
11) Digital thermometer

Brief Historical Events:

Three students taking the advanced ghost-hunting course at Lexington Community College provided me with the following history research on the Witches' Cemetery.

1) I did a little preliminary research and found a reference on the internet at the library. The cemetery we visited tonight is called the Hull Family Graveyard and is listed in the Fayette County Genealogical Society Quarterly v.2, no.2, p. 63, with inscriptions on pages 56 and 64.

Submitted by Tom Zumwalt

2) Here's some information on the cemetery we investigated last week I found in the Lexington Public Library downtown. I got this particular information from the "Fayette County Genealogical Society Quarterly" volume 2, number 2, page 63. I did all of my research in the Kentucky room—which is a room full of info on the history of Kentucky.

Jacob Hull, Jr. (30 years old) died on 7/4/1840
Mrs. Martha Hull 51 years old) died on 2/17/1845
wife of Jacob Hull, Sr.
Jacob Hull, Sr. (46 years old) died on 1/13/1834
Charles Hull (7 months & 6 days old) died on 10/1/1814
son of Jacob & Martha Hull
Elizabeth Jane Hull (21 years old) died on 7/2/1842
wife of Jacob Hull, Jr.
Charles McGowan died on 1/17/1842 (no age listed)
Elizabeth McGowan (68 years old) died on 1/13/1833
wife of Charles McGowan
John Key (48 years old) died on 1/12/1833

Submitted by Susan Rummel

3) I did some research on these names. The cemetery's real name is the Hull Family Cemetery or the McGowan Key Hull Cemetery. Once I had the last name of Charles, I was able to find a little more information. Charles McGowan was the father of Elizabeth and Nancy (didn't see her stone - could have been broken?). Nancy was married to John Key. I believe that this is the John Key who is buried there because the date he died was exactly the same as listed on the website. The McGowans were from Northern Ireland. Charles McGowan was married to Elizabeth Beard. I found a deed document where Charles McGowan and Elizabeth's brothers were named in the property transfer. Martha was married to Jacob Hull. It turns out that she died in 1845, not 1814. The "4" must have worn down. They had one child, Jacob. Martha's sister Nancy and John had six children, Mary Ann, Elizabeth, John Campbell, Charles Henry, Sally, and Louisa Jane.

Submitted by Pat Crowe.

Reported Witnessed Paranormal Occurrences:

The Witches' Cemetery is located on Nicholasville Rd., hidden by a thick growth of trees between Medical Heights and Ethan Allen. At first I thought it was owned by the city but later during our investigation a gentleman told us the cemetery belonged to the property of an apartment building directly behind the cemetery. He was curious as to what we were doing and said he belonged to the apartment complex neighborhood association and would appreciate any information we could find out about the cemetery, since no one there had a clue about it.

The reason for the name, I suspect, is that Wicca practitioners go to this small cemetery to meditate and they claim the energy there is incredible. They believe it is a portal and that they are able to reach great heights during the time they spend meditating there. They feel there are not only spirits that abound, but also other unknown entities.

Pre-Investigation findings:

I went to this cemetery around 5:00 p.m. one week before the class was to join me with a full investigation. I was only there about ten minutes and felt a hard pinch on my leg. At first I thought I had been bitten, but when the bruise came through there were no teeth marks, but a horizontal bruise as if I had been pinched instead. Shortly there after I got three voices on the recorder and my husband got some photos of the grave markers showing an object that resembles a coffin. It was purple with a blue outline. He also got a picture of me dowsing and there were two green mists within the shot above me. The energy was so strong I became dizzy within the next few minutes and we left. In only 30 minutes we got three voices and two great photos.

We went back in a couple of days for one more check and this time I went later in the evening, around 8:30. Again I noticed the energy that was present. We brought a writer who is doing a magazine article on ghost hunting and I was demonstrating what we do on a hunt for her article. I placed my recorder on the stone fence of the cemetery and we started to walk around. Since the place is so near the highway I started to explain all the different noises that would probably show up on the recorder. However, when I got home there was a noise I've never heard before. It almost sounded like one of those old fifties movies of a UFO landing. I sent the EVP to a couple of experts in the electronics field to see if there was a reasonable reason for me to get this sound and they couldn't really offer anything that fit the situation. We also got two great pictures of ectoplasmic mist coming off the ground. There was no mist there that night because the weather was clear and sunny. The mosquitoes were so bad we had to cut our investigation to about a half an hour. I felt really good at the results we got in that short period of time.

Paranormal Experience During the Investigation:

Before entering the small cemetery I led the group in asking permission for us to enter. I reminded the spirits/ghosts/entities that I had been there before and they had been very kind to me by providing great pictures and voices. After a few seconds 12 of us entered the small plot. Chuck Starr remained on the outside to film the event with a Sony nightshot camcorder.

Once entered, we gathered in a circle and bowed our heads and said a silent prayer, befitting each of our beliefs, for protection and a successful ghost hunt. We took our trash bags and started to clean the area of trash and debris. Then everyone started taking pictures and setting their recording devices while I surveyed the area with my TriField Natural EM meter. After noting the hot spots we continued to take photographs and record for EVPs.

The class was very eager to learn how to dowse for ghosts so I began a session for their benefit. I was able to contact a female spirit and gather information about her life. The time of death and age reflected one of the cemetery markers that someone found. I asked if she was that Martha. The rods responded, "yes." I then asked her if this had been a family plot and the rods responded, "yes." We recorded the information so we could see how close to the facts I would come after the class researched the cemetery.

Once I had finished the initial dowsing other students were in line to try. Again, we had great success and everyone who dowsed was able to pick up someone. There was a black man, a child and a white man with whom we talked. The all claimed to be buried there. This information will be valuable as we check the history.

Collected Evidence:

Photos:

1) Several orbs from different cameras, all 35 mm.
2) Two pictures with bright white cone-shaped anomalies.
3) Three dark shadows
4) A couple of faces in the bushes (but you know what they say about faces).

Videos:

A couple of orbs were recorded with the nightshot camcorder.

Audio Recordings:

1) Woman's voice, "Dust."
2) Male voice sound like a distant yell, "Hey Bill."
3) Female voice, "I would."
4) Female voice, "I've been here."
5) Female voice, "My dog's bones."
6) Female voice, "See, Yeah."
7) Old man's voice, "Thank you, kindly."

Comments:

After the research was collected we found out that the answer to all the questions I had asked Martha about she and her family were correct, except one. I asked her how many children she had and, with a yes and no response, we found that she had more than 5 but fewer than 10. According to the research in one document we found, she only had one son, Jacob. But in another document we found that she had two sons one of whom died at 7 months. Also, during my research of families in the 1800s I would find the names of daughters being born but never any mention of them getting married or when they died. Sometimes less mention of women was the case back then, because the emphasis was on the men's history as more important. So in answering my question about the children, if she had any female children who died young they may have not been listed. Or she could have had miscarriages and counted those as children.

Most of the voices we recorded were considered "C" quality with "A" being the best and "C" the worst. The traffic noise made it almost impossible to hear them speak, so I guess if we plan another trip there we should go around 3 o'clock in the morning so the traffic won't be so bad and the voices may come through a lot clearer.

Next to the tree a mysterious shape, looking like a coffin, was captured at the Witches' Cemetery (Hull Family Plot), in Lexington, Kentucky. Through our research we found that this was a family plot at one time. Back in the '50s they did bury some indigents in this small cemetery. Maybe this was a way for the spirit to let us know that someone was buried over them and they are not happy with that. Who knows? Photo taken by Chuck Starr.

This ectoplasmic mist is another indication that we may have caught a spirit form on film. This photo was taken at the Witches' Cemetery (Hull Family Plot), in Lexington, Kentucky by Patti Starr.

Anomaly. Photo by Patti Starr

Between the tree and Tory Eldridge, one of my students from Lexington Community College, notice the round white orb floating just above the ground. This photo was taken at the Witches' Cemetery (Hull Family Plot) in Lexington, Kentucky by Patti Starr.

This is another photo from the cemetery that shows tan orbs in two different places and surrounded by a bright light mist anomaly. Photo by Nancy Short.

Chapter 4

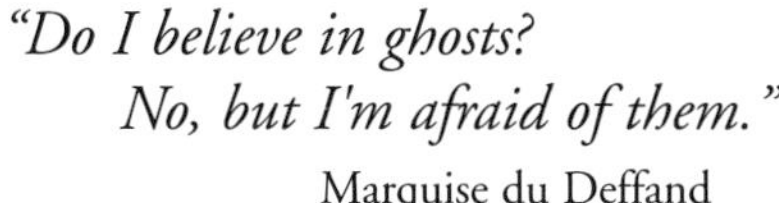

The Difference Between a Ghost & Spirit

"Do I believe in ghosts?
No, but I'm afraid of them."
Marquise du Deffand

I heard someone say, "I don't believe in ghosts but I'm scared to death of them." I've always felt that ghosts do exist. When I was a little girl, I used to talk to the little children who would come to my bed at night. Later, I had a few frightening experiences when a ghost came into my room and pulled at my covers as I had them over my head. Late one evening after going to bed, I had a conversation with my aunt who had committed suicide. So even though I was told that the children were a part of my imagination, that the ghost in my room pulling at my covers was a nightmare, and that I only thought I was awake when my aunt come to visit me after her death, I still knew in my heart that I had experienced ghosts.

Through my encounters and research of ghosts I have developed a couple of theories: Ghosts are different than spirits. Ghosts are entities that have died but don't realize they are dead. They refuse to cross over, go into the light, or go over to the other side. Because they stay earthbound, ghosts are the easiest of the spirits for us to see, hear, or feel. We are the intruders who show up in places that the ghosts continue to cling to as they did in life. After all, they were there first.

This is why they refuse to be quiet or leave when asked to go. Instead of fear, we should have compassion for them. We can certainly help them by talking and explaining to them that they are dead. That their lives here on earth are over. Tell them that they need to walk into the light where their loved ones are anxiously waiting for them. If that doesn't work, then pray for them each day that they may find their way into the light.

Spirits are different from ghosts in that they know they have died and now reside on the other side in the spirit realm. They come back to visit occasionally at happy times in our lives or in difficult times. They get great joy in coming back to see a grandchild graduate from college or a niece get married or to deliver an important message from the other side that might help in time of need. Spirits are a little kinder and subtler about their visits. Sometimes they make the recipient feel as though someone is watching them, as they might smell a favorite perfume or cigar smoke. Spirits may move a favorite book of theirs or move a picture of themselves out of place, just enough to be noticed. They will sometimes turn on clocks, lights, or televisions to get people's attention. Unlike ghosts, they will politely go away if you become scared or annoyed and ask them to leave. Spirits are not trying to frighten us. Rather, they just want to let us know that they are still with us and love us dearly.

Most of the stories about ghosts and paranormal happenings that I've written about throughout this book reflect my own personal experience. Every once in a while I will hear a really great first-hand story from one of my students or someone will send me through my email or website a story that happened to them, that I add to my own collection of experiences with ghosts. I have a couple that I wish to share with you. I have changed the names of the individuals to protect their privacy.

Rest in Peace

While driving home from work one evening, Jane noticed the car way out in front of her, had a tire blow out and the car started to swerve. Being an EMT and seeing her share of accidents, Jane figured that at the speed the car was going there was no way the driver was going to be able to safely pull over to stop, and she was right. To her horror she watched the car start to spin out of control and plunge over a steep embankment. Jane turned on her red light and pulled over to the spot where the car had gone over. Just as she was pulling off the road a state trooper approached her from the on-coming lane. He pulled off to join her to see what the problem was.

Jane was a little surprised that he would even have to ask what the problem was since he would have had to see the whole thing on his way up the same stretch of road. She told him how she watched the driver of this car lose control after a blowout and how it went over the embankment. The officer pointed out that there were no tire tracks on the road to indicate someone had skidded out of control.

With Jane still insisting that she had just witnessed a terrible accident they started to go down the steep embankment. They had walked a good distance and could see no signs that someone had just crashed their car into this area. Then all of a sudden the trooper thought he saw something reflect off his flashlight beam and to his shock, he realized that it was coming off a car. "Oh my God!" exclaimed the trooper, "There is a car down here. It looks like it slid down behind these tall bushes and crashed into a tree." They both started to move with haste to get to the car to remove the people before it caught fire. When they reached the car and shone the light to the driver's side they saw something that caused them both to jump back in shock. They did not find what most would expect from a bad accident. The person they saw was not injured nor covered in blood. Instead they saw a complete form of a skeleton. As they regained their senses they looked back into the car and noticed other abnormalities. There were leaves and pine needles all over the car and inside on the back and front seats. As they checked the area around where the car had rested there were no indentations on the grass and no bushes that should have been crushed on the car's way down. As the trooper turned his light back to the car he noticed something else that was out of the ordinary. The license plate had been expired for over a year.

The trooper called in for help and also for a check of the license plate number. He learned the car belonged to a woman who had been reported missing more than a year earlier. As the scene began to fill up with fire fighters, emergency teams, and a tow truck driver, everyone wanted to know how anyone could have found this car. Jane explained she was going home and saw the blowout take place right in front of her.

Once they pulled the car to the top of the embankment it was obvious that it did, indeed, have a blowout. All the pieces were coming together. The woman had been missing for a little over a year and the tags on her car had expired at about the same time. The only thing that didn't make any sense was that Jane had witnessed an accident that happened in that same spot over a year ago. Of course, everyone wanted to ask Jane so many questions about what she had seen, to try to make sense of what had just happened. After a couple of hours had passed and the last of the crews was leaving as the car was being towed away, the trooper commented on Jane's vision. He said he had heard of people who were receptive to psychic messages about this type of tragedy but he had never met one.

As Jane was saying her goodbyes to the trooper she turned to walk back to her car and as she did she heard a woman say, "Thank you, Darlin'." She turned to see who was behind her and all she saw was the trooper standing there with his mouth dropped open in shock. He told Jane that when he turned to watch her walk away he saw a woman walk up behind her and say, "Thank you, Darlin'," and disappear. A smile came over Jane's face and a sense of pride came through as she realized she had just helped a trapped soul become free. Now this spirit can rest in peace, she thought.

Justice Was Served!

Ashley's sister Sarah, was struggling with being a single parent and making her house payment, so Ashley decided to move in with her to help with these expenses. It was agreed that their quality of life would be so much better for both of them with this arrangement. To accommodate Ashley's living space, Sarah turned her walk out basement into a comfortable apartment with kitchenette, living room, office and bedroom. It made a great addition. Ashley's favorite part was the view she had through the sliding glass doors while standing in her living room over looking the beautiful lake front property. She knew she had made the right decision.

After a few days of settling in, Ashley began to notice strange things happening. She would experience cold spots in certain areas of the living room. She would check for drafts but couldn't locate any sources. All during the day and evening she would have the distinct feeling she was being watched, especially while watching TV. She would turn around quickly, expecting to see one of the children looking at her through the sliding glass doors, but there would be no one there. Sometimes when she would get this feeling the dog and cat would sit up and look over to the door as if they were expecting someone to walk in. When she would turn to see who had walked up to the door there would be no one there.

Things really started to get even stranger with the approach of winter. One evening while all alone in the house, Ashley decided to pop in a good movie, wrap up in a blanket, and enjoy a bowl of popcorn. It wasn't long into the movie that she began to get the strong feeling that she was being watched again. Once when the dog started to react as if someone had walked up to the glass doors she swung around for a look. To her shock she saw fog marks on the glass. She jumped up to check out what she thought she was seeing and, sure enough, she could make out impressions on the glass door that looked as though a small child had been pressing his nose, cheeks, and hands on the door. The outline was still very clear.

Thinking there might be someone trying to play a trick on her, she grabbed her coat and headed outside in the snow. She went upstairs to go out the front door so she could sneak around to the back and, hopefully, catch the prankster who had been coming up to her door. As she went around to the back of the house she noticed there were no footprints in the snow. She looked out across to the lake and saw there was nothing to indicate someone had walked up to the sliding-glass doors. As she was looking toward the water she saw that her rowboat had come loose and was being tossed out from the dock with the rope just barely hanging on. She went back inside for her gloves and hat, and returned to the windy, bitter cold outside to rescue her boat.

The storm that was blowing in had become stronger than she realized and the snow and wind were whipping at her face. As she faced the blur of snow hitting her face and eyes she was glad to see that the rope was still attached to the pier. She reached down to pull the rope up and just about halfway it became stuck and wouldn't move. Ashley was freezing at this point and with aggravation yanked the rope harder setting it free and she reeled the boat back in. As the boat came closer Ashley reached out very carefully to grab the bow, and just at that moment the rope was jerked back into the water causing her to lose her balance and fall headfirst into the boat. For a moment she was a little stunned but quickly regained her senses. Holding her head in her hands, she looked around to see what would have caught the rope and yanked it so hard. Unable to make out what had happened, she picked up the rope and started pulling herself and the boat back towards the pier. As she was nearing the pier all of a sudden the boat hit something under the water. As she tried to pull free she could hear a sound like metal being pulled over metal. She looked over the side and could see something close to the surface of the water, but couldn't quite make out what it was.

By now Ashley was upset and worried if she was ever going to make it back before she froze to death. She was determined to figure out what this thing was that had stopped her boat so she took off her glove and reached down into the icy waters. As her hand wrapped around the object she pulled it to the surface and could see that is was a yellow bicycle. It was an older model of a low rider with a banana seat and high handlebars. As she struggled to lift the bike into the boat she wondered why she had not noticed it before. She quickly pulled herself to the dock and once the boat was secured put the bike in the garage to show her sister in the morning. She returned to the warmth of her tidy abode, realizing how fortunate she was that she had not fallen into the lake. She thanked her lucky stars that she had landed in the boat, instead.

The next day, after Sarah and her boys came home, Ashley couldn't wait to tell her sister what had happened the night before. Just as she started to tell her, her four-year-old nephew, Connor, came running into the kitchen gibbering about a boy outside trying to get into the garage. Ashley and Sarah followed him back out to the garage to have a look. As they walked toward the garage Ashley continued to tell Sarah about this strange bike she had pulled out of the lake. When they got to the garage, there was no one there. They checked the area in the front and back of the garage and there were no footprints in the snow that would indicate a young boy had been present. Sarah told Ashley that Connor just had an over-active imagination and they went back into the house.

A week passed and Connor still was telling Ashley about this boy. He said the boy was very sad and scared, that he needed help and his name was Shane. Over the next few months, even Connor's sisters were talking about the boy, Shane, and they started including him in their games. One day a neighbor heard them outside playing in the snow, calling to Shane, and decided to call Sarah. It just so happened, she said, that in 1973 a young boy named Shane Austin who had lived in the house across the street had disappeared. She told them that the family had moved away in 1983 without a clue to what had happened to their son.

After Ashley heard the story she called the police and told them about the bike she had found and her nephew's story about the boy, Shane. She was surprised that the detectives were so open-minded and admitted that her nephew was probably communicating with Shane. The police went to the house and took the bike down to the police station. They took pictures of it, which they sent to the Austin family, to see if it was the same bike that belonged to Shane. They replied that it looked like the yellow 1971 Schwinn bike, with banana seat, that Shane had been seen riding before his disappearance. Ashley was shocked when she heard it was the missing boy's bike. The detectives were very dedicated to the case and kept the media from knowing about Connor's communications with Shane.

The police were not able to investigate the area any further while the waters were frozen so they waited until mid March to start the search again for the missing boy. During this time Connor would let Shane into the house and they would play for hours. We also started acknowledging Shane's presence and Connor insisted that Shane sleep with him on his top bunk. Though it became easier for them to feel Shane when he was around, only her nephew could communicate with him.

Connor told them that Shane was not sleeping well. He said Shane was having nightmares about a man named Harry. Connor said Shane was afraid to go into the shed across the street from where he used to live because Harry lived there and would hurt him if he went inside. Trying to make sense of it all, Ashley decided to confide in one of the investigating officers about what her little nephew had been telling them over the last few months. Once the officer went back and checked the files he found that the Austins did, indeed, have a gardener by the name of Harry. Earlier on in the investigation he had been listed as a suspect but was cleared because he had a good alibi, which was that he was working at another home the day Shane disappeared.

The police decided to go talk to Harry again and to check out his alibi one more time. They found a discrepancy in his story. Feeling the pressure from the detectives' constant questioning, Harry finally broke down and confessed to the murder of Shane Austin. He told the police that he had hidden in the shed of the Austins' home while the other workers went on to the next house. He knew that Mr. and Mrs. Austin would not be home until after 5 p.m., so he waited for Shane to arrive home on his bike. Right after Shane got home, Harry said he tried to lure him into the shed on the pretext of showing him some of his baseball cards. Once he got him inside he gagged him and tied him up. Then he molested him until, somehow, Shane was able to free himself and run away. He ran along the lakeshore trying to get to a neighbor's house for help when Harry caught up with him and dragged him into the water. During the struggle he drowned Shane. He took his body and wrapped it in a tarp and threw his bike into the lake. Harry told the police that he took the boy's body and buried it in the yard of the unfinished house across the street, which is now Sarah's house.

Sarah sent the children to their mother's house while the police dug up her back yard looking for the boy's body. It didn't take long for them to find him only twenty-five feet from Ashley's sliding glass doors—The very same doors where she had previously seen the fogged impressions of a child's hands and face pressed into the glass.

About an hour later, Sarah's mom called with a message from Connor. He wanted to tell them that Shane had to go home now and he wouldn't be coming back. From then on Ashley's nephew never mentioned Shane's name again.

Ashley figured that the police must have told the Austin family about Connor's ability to talk to Shane and through him they were able to break the case. Ashley received a lovely note from Shane's mother about how grateful she was that Ashley's family had been an important aid in clearing up the mystery of her son's death. She said she felt sure that Shane was finally at peace once given a proper burial with his family present to say their final goodbyes, and that justice was served.

Chapter 5

Ghost Theories

"If you believe in ghosts, proof is not necessary. If you don't believe in ghosts, proof doesn't matter."
Patti Starr

Could ghosts be the disincarnate souls of the dead? Are they just memory images stamped on the atmosphere of places like pieces of old film? Could it be that they are simply masses of electromagnetic energy expelled into our environment when the electrical charges of the human hosts cease to function? You can get so many different answers to the question, "What are ghosts?" Some say they are spirits of the dead that are earthbound, while others claim that ghosts are nothing more than our imaginations. The answers vary from guardian angels to demonic entities.

In theory, ghosts are the remains of disembodied human beings. They maintain their personalities and same intelligence they had when they were alive, but now they exist without the hosts we call human bodies. They continue on as spirits of thought, reasoning, emotions, ego, and other traits that make up the human psyche.

I've included some theories about ghosts and the spirit world in this material. Remember, these are theories and not facts and there are exceptions to every rule. That's why they are called theories.

Ghost stories filled folklore long before historians began writing down the most popular ghost tales and legends. Here we are, in the new millennium and still hearing reports of spectres and ghostly phenomena. What is out there that so many of us are seeing, hearing and experiencing? Why is there so much interest in the study of ghostly phenomena?

Children and Spirits

Have you ever wondered how some children can be so sincere while talking to or about an imaginary friend? Children seem to see and sense what most adults either cannot or will not see. Babies and children do not know what is supposed to be, so their perception of a spirit is more finely tuned than most adults. Wanting to protect their children, the parents tell them, it was just a bad dream, or there are no such things as ghosts, or it's only your imagination. Explanations like these will teach and reinforce children to block these images and senses. As they get older they soon lose this ability to see and communicate with these spirits. I've often heard mothers say, "The doctor told me not to worry about their imaginary friend, because they will eventually grow out of it." They grow out of it because they are conditioned not to trust their inner selves.

Since the child is the only one in the family to recognize the spirit, it is no wonder that it chooses to interact with the child. These spirits or ghosts tend to protect the child and become its friend. Maybe we should pay more attention to these friends of theirs. When I'm called to investigated a home that is supposedly haunted, the first thing I want to know is, if they have a small child and if so, if the child has an imaginary friend.

Intelligence of Orbs

Orbs are globe-shaped lights of energy caught on film, usually during a haunting or paranormal experience, and thought to be the forms of ghosts or spirits. An orb is made up of the life force that powered its former human body. Why does it appear in the shape of an orb? Think of it like this: say the spirit could form a barrier around its energy (as air in a bubble), the energy gently pushes against all the sides equally, causing an orb shape as the result. The spirit may also have control over size and density. Why couldn't several orbs come together and form one large orb for support in times of distress or for strength? I have witnessed this phenomenon through some of my own photos.

While I was on a haunting investigation in a friend's house, I had a feeling that I should take a picture of the ceiling. Just as I took the picture and the flash went off, I saw an orb fly across the ceiling with a red streak behind it. It was the first time I had seen an orb with my naked eye. Excitedly, I told everyone there what I had just seen. The next day when I picked up the pictures, sure enough, I had captured on film exactly what I saw and described to my friends.

I've also learned that I get better results on film if I ask the ghosts or spirits for permission to take their pictures. In another investigation, I decided to ask the spirits to take the shape of shields instead of orbs so I could prove that I was communicating with them and that they understood me. When I picked up my pictures, I found shield-shaped images on my film, instead of the orbs. A lady I met via the internet sent me copies of photos she had just made with her digital camera. She said when she got orbs on the first two shots, she also asked the spirits to take the shape of shields and the next photo showed a shield instead of an orb.

From these experiences, I've come to the conclusion that orbs are intelligent spirits and they decide when and how they want to be photographed.

Living Alone with Visitors of Light

Years ago, when I was a single mom living alone with my nine-month old son, I experienced some pretty spine-tingling experiences while living in a little duplex nestled back against our community's golf course. Shortly after we had moved in strange things started happening. While sitting on the sofa in the evenings, I would feel a cold draft sweep across my shoulders as though I had a window open. But, there were no open windows and since it was early spring no air-conditioning.

When these cold drafts would occur my little dog Brigitte would whine and shake while she stared down the hall. When I would turn to glance myself I would see a flickering light as though I had left a candle burning, which was not the case. Sometimes, I would look up and see balls of light pass quickly over my head and disappear down the hall. During this period of my life, I knew nothing about orbs so I was a little concerned about what was going on.

I noticed that when Brigitte would start whining I could hear a movement like someone walking or shuffling their feet. When I would turn to look, I could see nothing, but could hear the footsteps coming down the hall. As the sound grew louder, Brigitte would jump onto the sofa and bark towards the hall. Time and time again, I would get up to check out the disturbances and check on the baby but I would find nothing out of the ordinary.

One night I was awakened by Brigitte, who was whining and yelping in the middle of my bedroom. When I sat up in my bed, I noticed that my door was closed. I thought this was strange since it was my habit not to close it. My baby was in the bedroom across the hall and I needed to be able to hear him should he awake. Before I could get out of bed, I saw a light flickering and shining under the door as voices and footsteps kept coming closer.

Fear set in and I didn't know what to do. My phone was in the kitchen so I couldn't call the police. I was shaking so hard I could barely walk, but I managed to get to the door so I could hear what was going on. I picked up a lamp that I had made out of a wine bottle and took the shade and attachment off, to use the bottle as a weapon. I was convinced that someone was in my house and this bottle was all I had to protect my child and me. I heard a woman's voice clearly and distinctly call out my son's name. "Shane, Shane," and without any thoughts of consequences I put my hand on the doorknob to rush out to see who was in my house. At that exact moment a big bang hit against the door with such force I jumped backwards. Instead of fear I felt rage and yelled out, "You are not getting my baby," as I threw open the door and drew back the bottle in my hand. As I stood there with weapon lifted, all I could see was a dark hallway and a dim light coming from a small night light in my son's bedroom. I immediately turned on the hall light and looked to see if anyone was moving down at the other end. I rushed into my son's room and found him sound asleep. I looked around his room and there was nothing out of place and Brigitte had stopped barking.

My knees felt like they were made of rubber and I was shaking, but found the courage to walk down the hall and call the police. The police came and they checked the entire house and surroundings. They assured me that no one could have been in my house because all the doors and windows were locked from the inside and they found no evidence of anyone being around the outside of the house. I wanted them to believe me about the lights, voices and the bang on the door, but they just looked at each other. They did, however, promise to drive by for the next couple of days to check my place to make sure everything looked normal.

I lived there for almost a year and I had many more unexplained experiences, among them were visions and conversations with relatives that had passed over and a premonition that one of my friends would be severely injured in a car accident. Years later, with a lot of experiences and research behind me, I would be convinced that the duplex must have been built over a portal and that is why I had such strange paranormal encounters.

Afraid of the Dark

"Momma, please don't close the door. I'm afraid of the dark," came the plea from her six-year-old daughter, as Eunice put her down for the evening. "Now, Patti, you know that you have no reason to be afraid of the dark. Jesus is in the room with you and he is not going to let anything bad happen to you," replied her mom. As she closed the door she heard Patti say in a tiny quivering voice, "Jesus, I know you are in here because my Momma said you were, but please don't move or you will scare me to death." Though this story has brought many a chuckle, one question still remains. Why was Patti so frightened of the dark? Why are any of us frightened of the dark? Could it be because we fear unknown sounds and movement, as our imaginations tell us that there may be ghosts around us? At least, that's what people have been saying since the earliest of times.

Light makes most of us feel safe and that's why I use a prayer for light to surround the group with the energies of all positive forces to protect and keep all negative energies from us while we are doing our ghost investigations. In my many years of searching for ghosts I have yet to run into an evil or demonic force, so the prayers must work. Or maybe there are no demonic and evil ghosts out there. Maybe they are just angry or upset about an untimely death. It could be that when they were alive they had a mean or hateful personality that has carried over with them to the other side. They could be desperately trying to get our attention by moving objects, slamming doors, or occasionally hitting or pinching us. I'm not trying to say that there are no such things as evil or demonic entities, but I am saying, the odds of finding evil or demonic ghosts are far less than people realize.

When I'm asked what message I hope to give people from all my investigations, I say that I hope to re-educate them about ghosts and spirits. To let them know that the Hollywood version of ghosts and spirits as being demonic is over-rated. Of course, I like a really good scary ghost story just like the next person. I can remember my all time favorite movie being "Poltergeist" and the next being "Sixth Sense." These are fantastic movies and some of the experiences in both movies are very possible, while other parts are only fiction. We just need to realize what is real. Of course, ghost hunting is not an exact science, therefore not considered real to the scientific community and skeptics. But then, that is what makes our world even more interesting. Wouldn't it be a boring place to live if we were all alike, if we were all the same color, were the same religion, had the same beliefs, and had the same taste in clothes, homes, and cars. It's variety that keeps life so interesting and learning to respect and appreciate all these differences in our culture is a wonderful global goal.

Chapter 6

Ghosts & the Old Hag

"I look upon death to be as necessary to our constitution as sleep. We shall rise refreshed in the morning."

Benjamin Franklin

Sleep paralysis or the "Old Hag" is a phenomenon known in almost every culture in the world. It is a condition in which someone, most often while lying on their back, just before dropping off to sleep or just waking up, realizes that they cannot move, speak or cry out. Once the person realizes that they are unable to move, a whole gamut of hallucinations may occur. Some people swear that it was an "Old Hag" of a woman sitting on their chest holding them down or an alien sitting on them and holding them down or the devil with his helpers holding them down. Others say they felt crushed, smothered, or pushed into the bed. Many suffering from an occasional episode of this condition were convinced that a ghost or demon haunted their bedroom.

It has been just recently, within the last 10 years, that researchers have begun studies about this bizarre condition. Researchers at University of Waterloo, Ontario, Canada, have done some of the most intense research on sleep paralysis (SP). They have found some interesting facts about the REM dream state. While we are dreaming in a normal REM state, our mind sends out a message to our body to cease our normal motor functions. Our muscles turn off in a sense, so that we do not act out our dreams. For some reason instead of following REM and going into a deep sleep state the person wakes up and regains consciousness but continues to dream. The paralysis is due to the failure of the brain neurons to remind the body that it is now awake, so it is unable to move. The scary part is that the person is not only unable to move, but also dreaming while awake, a condition that is very confusing and frightening. The hallucinations that take over seem very real and they feel their life is threatened.

There are two major types of sleep paralysis. One is called common sleep paralysis and the other is hallucinatory sleep paralysis.

According to most researchers nearly every adult will have an episode of common sleep paralysis once every couple of years. Through targeted research they discovered that sometimes sleepers gain consciousness and find their bodies temporarily frozen. This temporary paralysis affects the gross motor functions and macro muscle groups of the body. This state lasts from fifteen seconds to a minute, and is the most common duration. Though waking to this helpless state can be disturbing for the individual, it is perfectly harmless and fairly common.

A more terrifying type of sleep paralysis is called hallucinatory sleep paralysis also known as the hypnagogic sleep paralysis and the hag phenomenon. There are three major differences between common sleep paralysis (CSP) and hallucinatory sleep paralysis (HSP). The first is that CSP is common and universal, while HSP is rare and seems to be geographically episodic. The second is that CPS is of relatively short duration while HSP can last as long as seven to eight minutes. The third and a major difference in that CSP may be unsettling for the sleeper, but HSP can be horrible, as it is commonly accompanied by a nightmarish hallucination.

There is some evidence that HSP seems to affect certain population areas as if it were an epidemic. A region that has had no HSPs reported can all of a sudden have several. These areas can remain infected for up to three years; the most common duration is only a few months. There is no explanation for this, as of yet.

The most outstanding difference between HSP and CSP is the

horrifying hallucination that accompanies the paralysis. The source of the hallucination has often been attributed to the hypnagogic state (the state between wakefulness and sleep). An individual usually awakens either because they hear something or they feel something. The thing to remember is that this occurs outside of a dream sequence plot. The individual is wide-awake yet paralyzed, as in CSP. Moments after the person has awakened they are startled by a terrifying visual hallucination. The horrific form is usually a small malevolent creature that straddles the victim and attempts to strangle them or sit on their chest to prevent them from breathing. Most victims are convinced that the creature was trying to kill them.

When I get a phone call from someone who says that their house has a horrible demon that attacks them at night, my first thought is that it might be sleep paralysis. Then when they describe the experience and where they are possessed and can't move, or say something hideous is sitting on their chest and they can hardly breath, I conclude that it is not a ghost or demon but most probably sleep paralysis. When I tell them that their experience may have something to do with a sleep condition they become very defensive and want to convince me that in no way was it a dream or their imagination. Then I go into detail and explain to them what SP means and most of the time I can reassure them that the house is probably ok. I also advise them to educate themselves on this phenomenon, and in the meantime to try to sleep on their side. Sleep paralysis very rarely occurs when you sleep in that position.

Night Terrors

Another very frightening sleep disorder is called night terrors, which usually occur in the first half of the night, in the fourth (non-REM) cycle of sleep. The afflicted will wake up screaming and crying with terrified looks on their faces reflecting the horror they are experiencing. The victim doesn't say anything and will usually flail around out of control. The sleeper is completely unaware of their surroundings and seems immune to being consoled or calmed down. There is no dream or nightmare causing this terror.

The victim has dilated pupils, can hyperventilate and experience sweating during this time. These episodes can last from one to fifteen minutes. Once the victim has regained orientation, they fall back to sleep almost immediately. It is very rare that a person will remember any of the event in the morning.

Despite thirty years of researching sleep disorders, the exact cause of night terrors remains unknown. What most researchers will agree on is that night terrors result from a disruption in the normal stage of slow wave sleep cycle. There is evidence that children suffering from emotional disorders, developmental disorders, or recent traumatic events, have a higher incidence of night terror attacks. Some believe there is a connection between fatigue and night terrors. More recent studies show a link between violent TV shows and incidences of night terrors.

Veronica's Story

One morning as I was reading my emails I came across a message from a stranger named Veronica that touched my heart. She started out by telling me that her father had committed suicide and wasn't found until nine days later. After he was cremated the family took his ashes to his favorite fishing spot in hopes that he would find peace as they washed his ashes down the Chattahoochee River. While they were there, a friend took a picture of them releasing the ashes. When they got the pictures developed they saw some strange anomalies in their photos. Veronica described them as misty swirls with a heart-shape within the swirls. She asked me if this could have anything to do with her dad. She said she really didn't believe in ghosts, but this had her wondering. Veronica wanted me to take a look at her photos and give her my opinion of what they might be.

I sent a reply right away and told her how sorry I was to hear about her father's passing. I told her that if she was willing to share the full account of what happened to her father with me, I was willing to listen. More information would help me determine what was going on in the photos.

She agreed and sent me the picture with the heart-shaped

anomaly and the following story. Her dad and mother got a divorce when Veronica was twelve years old. During the next few years her dad was in and out of her and her brother's lives, with little development in their relationships. He was a difficult person to get close to and had a knack of pushing away from him the people that loved him the most. It was not until after she and her brother were grown and had children of their own that their dad started coming back around again. Sometimes life with him would be very good and then sometimes he would become upset over something and stop speaking to them and go off on his own again. She admitted that he made it very difficult to love him, though she did love him dearly.

Her dad was always jumping from job to job as a skilled laborer. About seven years ago he had fallen from a building and severely injured his back. He received a large settlement a few years later from workman's compensation and was able to make up for some bad times with his kids by giving them a part of the settlement. He told them that he wanted to give them their inheritances early so he could watch them enjoy the money. Her dad bought a mobile home and left Alabama to be closer to them and live on his son's land.

On February 2, 2001, her dad called her and asked if she would call the phone company to get his phone connected to his new place. She told him that she was really busy taking registrations for baseball at the time and she might not have time to do it that day but would call the next day, for sure. He settled for that, said goodbye and Veronica told him that she loved him before hanging up. Those were her last words to him and the last time she would ever hear from her dad again.

The very same day that her dad called her, he also called her brother and was upset and very cross with him. The conversation didn't last long and Veronica and her brother figured that they would not be hearing from him for a while. Once he got mad at either one of them it could be a few days, a week or even six months before he would call or come around again.

On February 11, 2001 while Veronica was getting ready for church her brother came over to see if she had heard from their dad. They had just figured that their dad was still brooding over a disagreement, and didn't give it much thought. Their cousin came by and he also asked about their dad. He was a disabled Vietnam War veteran and visited their dad regularly. When they told him that he had gotten upset and hadn't called or come by to see them, he figured their dad was just being himself. When their cousin left to go home he got about half way there and decided to stop and check on their dad. When he reached out to knock on the door, he could smell a scent of death. A smell that was familiar with him, being a former medic in Vietnam.

When Veronica got the message that her father was dead her world turned upside down and she went immediately to her dad's house. His oxygen was still on, and he was almost unrecognizable with his weight going from 130 pounds to over 200 pounds. When she heard that he had killed himself with a gunshot wound to the head she was devastated.

Veronica's brother wanted to take his father's ashes to his favorite fishing place even though he had not been able to go there in a while due to advanced illness. It was a long walk down, alongside a creek, where it eventually runs into the Chattahoochee River. They went there the weekend that would have been their father's 63rd birthday to scatter his ashes on a favorite rock were he loved to stand and trout fish. They thought this would make a great final resting place for their dad, as they splattered water on the rock to wash his ashes down the river.

During the ceremony a friend who waited on the bank took pictures and unknowingly captured a strange anomaly in a couple of the pictures. It was a misty form of swirls and a heart shape just over Veronica as she poured out the ashes. She told me that no one was smoking and there was no campfire. It was a beautiful, clear, sunny day, so perfect for what they had to do. Veronica said when she saw the pictures she immediately thought it was her dad's spirit surrounding them.

As I viewed the photo a wonderful feeling came over me and I felt that the swirls were her dad's way of showing them that he was so happy now and all the pain and sorrow were gone and his spirit was free. He was free to soar, fly, dance around them in the pure light of love that he had shone down on them in the picture. They had made him even more happy by casting his ashes into a beautiful natural paradise where the water was clear and the area was green with foliage and flowers. It seemed that he was there with them and wanted them to know how much he appreciated their kind act of love. When looking up the word heart in the dictionary, I found love, devotion and courage as part of the defination. Since these words could not be spoken by Veronica's dad, he was able to show them in the photo his message with this single white heart.

Since her dad's passing, at times Veronica has felt a strong presence around her. She has seen lights float across the room out of the corner of her eye, but just as she would turn there would be nothing there. At times, she has felt him rub her, the way he had when he was alive. When she wrote to me again about these experiences I explained to her the difference between ghosts and spirits. I told her that in her dad's case, he was probably visiting her as a spirit and not a ghost that is bound to earth and can't go on. He wants to gently let her know that once in a while he is with her. As time passes his visits will most likely get fewer but I told her for a while to enjoy his time with her. I suggested to her that if she thinks her dad is near, he probably is and she can talk to him if it makes her feel better. Let him know that he is loved and she is happy that his suffering is over and that he is in a much better place. Consider it a blessing that she has the gift of knowing when her dad is with her and sensitive to his presence, I told her.

All in all these suggestions did make Veronica feel better and eased her fears that her dad's ghost was haunting her. Just when I thought I had helped Veronica put her life back together she wrote me again about some disturbing dreams that she was having about her dad. They upset her so badly that she thought he was being mean to her and she didn't know what to do or how to handle what was happening to her.

She said that before falling asleep she would feel unusually stressed and as though something was going to happen to her. She would have these disturbing dreams that her dad had come into the room with her and sat down on the bed beside her. She is convinced

Just over Veronica's brother and little girl is a heart shape mist forming around them as they scattered their dad's ashes into his favorite fishing place. It was a very emotional moment for everyone that day. It seems that their dad was very pleased at this ritual of love and this is how he was able to show them. A friend stood on the side and took this photo while they emptied his ashes. There was one more photo with swirling mist but the rest of the photos taken that day were perfectly clear of any mist.

that she wakes up, but is paralyzed and can't move. She sees that her dad is still sitting with her on the bed and the fact that she knows he is dead, makes her want to scream, but nothing will come out. She can't move or find the breath to scream and she tries with all her might to sit up, but can't. She knows that she is not asleep and she feels like her dad is purposely trying to scare her and she can't figure out why. The fear she feels is so consuming that she thinks she is going to die and maybe that is what her dad is trying to do. He has come back to take her with him and she is not ready to go. As she continues her struggle she can feel herself being able to move and gain control over her body once again, so she sits up and looks straight ahead just as her dad disappears before her eyes.

As I already knew about the recent loss of her dad and the terrible way he met his fate I could understand the stress that Veronica was going through. The experience that she was having at night, while sleeping, sounded very much like a sleep paralysis condition. I sent her a segment of the chapter I wrote on this condition and advised that she try meditation before falling asleep and not to sleep on her back. I also advised her that if she continued to have these dreams she should seek a sleep clinic.

After reading the explanation of sleep paralysis Veronica agreed that what I had told her made sense. She said the experience felt so real it made her feel as though a very unnatural force was causing her this discomfort, but that it was easier to believe the sleep paralysis conclusion, instead. She promised herself she would not go to sleep on her back again.

Veronica stays in touch and tells me that her dad is still around. Usually when she feels him the cabinet doors in the kitchen will open and close three times. Even her husband, when she is not home, will hear the cabinet doors open and close three times as though this is his signal that he's in the house. When these doors open and close even their little dog, Rambo, will stand up and look into the kitchen. Sometimes he'll bark and other times he will refuse to go into the kitchen. Veronica thinks her dad is teasing the dog and is having fun doing so.

Usually most of my investigations result in my going into the home of someone with these kinds of disturbances. I was lucky enough to help Veronica figure out what was going on in her home and her life without actually having to be there. She continues to email me and keeps me updated on her recovery from her loss. She is being a real trooper in facing her trials, with a real desire to learn the lessons life has offered her. The picture of this perfect white heart suspended over her and her brother as they empty their dad's ashes into a river hidden in a panoramic paradise scene gives her the comfort she needs, knowing that her dad was there and validated his love and presence in a photo.

Chapter 7

Where To Find Ghosts

"Everything in nature is resurrection, and it is not more surprising to be born twice than once."
Voltaire

In the Tibetan Book of the Dead, once a spirit accepts death of the physical body, it discovers a new one that makes travel a remarkable wonder. It can travel anywhere in seconds, through rock walls or mountains with ease. If the spirit wishes to be somewhere, it can arrive there in a thought.

Ghosts have no physical margins. Their ability to travel is limitless and they can be anywhere at any time. Although there is no scientific proof for suggesting that a location of longevity produces ghosts, historically, older places have proven to produce the best results when looking for a ghost. Maybe, the older the place is, the longer the duration of time in which different events could lead to a haunting. Also, these older locations can provide a familiar place to a ghost. Sometimes a ghost will be drawn to what is familiar. As we advance into a more modern future, our world changes around them making their surroundings less familiar. This may cause them to retreat to a place that has undergone little change and gives them more comfort. That's why I feel I get great results when looking for ghosts in old historic buildings. It is possible to find a ghost that has been there from the beginning or a ghost that has just recently taken up residency because of the ambience.

Listed below are places where you will most likely find ghosts:

1) Residences of friends and relatives are good places to start a ghost hunt. It doesn't have to be an old residence. Sometimes the most haunted house can be a brand new one. It's not the house the spirit hangs on to, but its location.
2) Schools and colleges may attract ghosts because of all the energy given off by the young people there. Some schools will survive a tragic event that may draw ghosts of teachers, students, or janitors.
3) Hospitals are a great source, but you may have a hard time doing an investigation or getting permission to do so. I'm sure you can understand why they would not want the added stress of ghost stories to their patients' lives.
4) Cemeteries that have history of hauntings are an excellent choice for ghost hunting. Also, if you can find a smaller or less visited site, the spirits are more anxious to show them selves, since they don't see many visitors.
5) Hotels sometimes host spirits of people dying there while traveling away from home. They could have died of natural means, suicide, drowning in a hot tub, or from falling off a balcony.
6) Theaters tend to lure all types of ghosts, especially those who were involved in theater as a career. Some ghosts are summoned there by the high energy of the living performers.
7) A library is a place where it is calm and serene. The spirits are found here because they enjoy passing through the books and can get lost in the reading.
8) Churches seem to be another successful place to find a lingering soul. It is a place to give them comfort and they can feed off the positive energy through the congregation's singing. Remember to look for the spirits in your photographs when you take pictures of weddings or other events.

9) Crime scenes and battlefields are locations filled with tragedy. Dying before their time may keep ghosts lingering behind, confused, not knowing they have died. Sometimes the negative energy imprints the memory and becomes a residual haunting. This results in the horrific events replaying over and over in the same area.
10) Museums are a good place to start to find a spirit. With all the antiques and old furnishings, you sometimes will find an item that has a ghost attached to it. Museums offer a quiet and serene place for a spirit to stay behind and lock into a certain period of time.

Case Study Report Ditto House

This is an example of what could happen when you are looking for a place to investigate, and the spirits find a way to you. While taking part in the Bourbon Festival, in Bardstown KY, I was asked to do the ghost tours, "Spirits in the Night," spirits being a play on words, considering it was a bourbon affair. During both nights of the tour I had someone within the group ask me if I had ever investigated the "Ditto House," in West Point, KY. As chance would have it, I met the owners of this noted haunted house, Mr. and Mrs. Steve Conley, on the last ghost tour. Steve asked me if I could bring my group to the Ditto House and do a complete investigation before they moved in, since he had just purchased the property. Steve belongs to a ghost-hunting group from Louisville, KY, known as the Louisville Ghost Hunters Society, with Keith Age as president/founder. Keith is also a Kentucky representative of the American Ghost Society and had already conducted a ghost hunt with Steve at the Ditto House earlier that week.

Steve was interested in seeing if another group would get the same results or find something different. Since I'm one of the few ghost hunters who dowse during an investigation, Steve was curious about what I might find with my dowsing ability. I have included a full report with the results of this investigation.

Ghost Chaser International
Case Study Report of Paranormal Activity

Case #: 517

Report Submitted by: Patti Starr

Description of Location: The Ditto House, West Point, Kentucky

Date: September 25, 2001 **Day:** Tuesday

Time In: 6:00 p.m. **Time Out:** 8:00 p.m.

Weather: Sunny Temp.: H 57/ L 41

Humidity: 93%
Barometric: 30.07 & Rising
Solar Rays: X class flare
Geomagnetic Field: Quiet
Lunar Phase: day after the first Quarter

Investigators Present:

1) Patti Starr
2) Chuck Starr
3) Bill Bailey
4) Lori Baker
5) Pat Crowe
6) Susan Rummel

Spectators Present:

1) Steve Conley
2) Keith Age
3) Carrie Galloway
4) Greg Crawford

List of Equipment & Devices:

1) Cannon 35 mm camera
2) Easy Shot 35 mm camera
3) Polaroid 35 mm camera
4) Film Kodak Gold, 400 speed
5) Nikon 950 digital camera
6) Sony 700X Digital Zoom Steady Shot
7) TDK HI8 120 MP Premium video tape
8) RCA 50X Digital Zoom Auto Shot
9) Maxell HGX-Gold 30 video tape
10) Sony mini cassette audio recorder with external mic
11) General Electric mini cassette audio recorder with external mic
12) Sony regular tape audio recorder with external mic
13) Gauss EMF meter
14) TriField Natural EM Meter
15) Laser beam light
16) Compass
17) Dowsing rods
18) Thermal Scanner

Brief Historical Events:

Ditto House Inn Bed and Breakfast, constructed in the Federal style, was restored in 1985, after serving as a private residence, a primitive bank, a ticket agency, a boarding house, and a Civil War hospital and barracks for General William T. Sherman. It is quite common to find buttons, coins, belt buckles, and other items in the general area, left behind by the troops. Other homes in the town are also on the Historic Register, including a "Sears and Roebuck" house, ordered from the catalog and delivered on the railroad. The Ditto House is a brick structure whose exterior walls are 18 inches thick. The woodwork, banisters, staircase, and upstairs floors are all original.

Submitted by Lori Baker:

The Ditto House is built on the location of the first cabin built in West Point. John Shields traded a cow for the land and a primitive cabin in 1798. The oldest part of the present building was built in 1841. In 1850, the Guthrie brothers bought the building and turned it into a boarding house and a primitive bank. Elm Street was a cobblestone road known as the Louisville-Nashville turnpike. In the 1870s, the building was used as a ticket office for the I.C. Railroad. The Ditto House received its name from Abraham and Ella Ditto, who bought the house and used it as a hotel and restaurant during the 1880s and 1890s.

Since that time, it has been used for a house of ill repute and a hospital during the Civil War. Everything past the kitchen has been built on since the 1890s.

Reported Witnessed Paranormal Occurrences:

The Ditto House is an old Federal-style home located in West Point, KY. In 1985, shortly after Carol and Cookie Goldsmith bought it, they began to hear noises up in the attic. It sounded like trunks or big boxes being moved around. The noises would occur in the middle of the night, around 2 a.m. seemed to be coming from a wall down the hallway. This went on for months.

Some nights it would sound like two women arguing in high-pitched voices. The Goldsmiths couldn't make out what was being said, but said sometimes it almost sounded like they were calling out their names. This went on for about a month until one night they heard the voices coming into their bedroom and continuing to argue as they circled the bed.

Another time, around Christmas, while Carol was lying in bed she felt a presence of someone staring at her. As she turned her head she saw a redheaded woman looking around the door frame at her. She was dressed in period clothing of the 1900s and seemed disturbed about something. Carol called for her husband and just as she did, the apparition disappeared.

The next time Carol saw the redheaded woman was about a month later in the same bedroom. This time she was standing at the foot of her bed, with her hands on her hips looking down at Carol as she lay in bed. No sooner did Carol's feet hit the floor, than the apparition disappeared.

During the same time of these events, Carol and Cookie would return home at night to find the lights on, dishes turned upside down, and mirrors turned toward the wall.

Another incidence which happened to their housekeeper caused the woman to quit her job. One day as she went downstairs and turned to walk back to the kitchen, she was stunned to see an old gray-haired man with a long white beard sitting on the couch. She said he wore a gray Civil War uniform, with a high collar and rows of buttons. When she realized what she was seeing she ran out the back door and never went back to work again.

The house was sold to Sherry and Mickey Dale in 1998. Shortly after moving in they had their first ghostly experience. It was about 1a.m. and Sherry was asleep on the daybed and Mickey had just fallen asleep in their regular bed. Mickey was startled awake by heavy boot steps coming up the stairs to their bedroom. He grabbed a flashlight and shone it in the direction of the steps which were coming closer to his bed, but he could not see anything. He felt it might have been the old Civil War soldier about whom he had heard.

In the year 2000, Sherry rented two of the upstairs rooms for a couple of months to a young couple with two daughters. Unaware of any of the ghost stories with them they had their first encounter early one September morning. While the mother was outside playing with her two girls she decided it was time to go back into the house. With both her daughters by her side she started up the stairs when she smelled the scent of strong, pipe smoke. When she got to the top of the stairs she noticed the door to the girls' room was open. She remembered closing it before going outside. Glancing into the room from the hallway she was shocked to find a man lying on the bed with his hands behind his head and his feet crossed. She could see the pipe smoke encircling his head and noticed that he was wearing dark, rough-looking clothes. She said he turned his head and looked right at her for a few seconds and then disappeared right before her eyes. Shortly after this, the renters moved away.

Pre-Investigation findings: N/A

Paranormal Experience During the Investigation:

When we got to the Ditto House I asked the new owners, Steve and Melody Conley, not to tell me about any of the ghostly events that had been going on in the house or any of the stories that had been told over the last few years. I wanted to see what I would pick up from my dowsing. They agreed and we started setting up our equipment. We had a crew of 6 investigators with us; all of them had graduated from the ghost-hunting course I taught at Lexington Community College. The team which included Bill Bailey, Lori Baker, Pat Crowe, Susan Rummel, along with Chuck Starr and Patti Acord Starr; president of Ghost Chasers International, proceeded to investigate this 1800s bed and breakfast home.

As I started to set up my video cameras, Pat immediately started getting orbs with her digital camera. The first ones were over my head as I was trying to set up all the equipment. Once she let everyone know where the activity was being documented, I set up both my EMF meter and TriField Natural EM meter, which started registering immediately. Now this house was empty and the new owners were not moving in for another week so there were not a lot of appliances around to disturb these fields. All the electrical wiring in this house is enclosed in conduit. There is no wiring inside any of the walls, but there is a small amount of wiring in the ceiling in the rear of the house in the newer addition. Pat continued to take snapshots with her digital and during the investigation recorded over 30 orbs. The rest of us were getting a few orbs, as well. We were using 35 mm and a digital camera of Lori's, that was getting some of the same orbs as Pat's.

I had a very strange experience as I put film into my Cannon 35 mm. I was pulling my film out across the teeth of the inside of my camera so the film would advance once I closed the film-loading door. All of a sudden the film started loading on its own and was being pulled out of the cartridge. I had to slam the door shut before all my film was exposed. It was so weird. The other members heard the commotion and asked me, what I did. I told them I had no idea how my film could advance like that. The door was all the way opened while I was loading my film and only when the door is closed should the film advance. This was just the beginning of our equipment acting strange and mal-functioning.

More problems with the equipment involved the audiocassette recorders. I set up my recorder first testing my voice, which came through okay, and I placed it on the window sill in one of the main rooms. I was about to set up my second recorder and during testing my voice sounded a little wobbly and strange. I figured the batteries were drained, so I changed them to new ones. Even though I changed the batteries, my voice still sounded a little wobbly, but I went ahead and started the recorder and attached the mic to my collar.

When I got home and started to listen to the recordings I chose the first tape from the recorder whose mic I had attached to my collar. While dowsing I usually get voices that come through as they answer my yes and no questions. At the beginning of this recording my voice was fine and I picked up some strange whispering, but as the tape continued my voice got a little faster and faster until I could not make out anything I said. I tried setting it at different settings, but it did not help. I even switched to another recorder and the tape sounded the same. Being so disappointed, I was hoping that I would get something from the stationary recorder that I had left in one of the rooms. It started out the same way with a few whispers and then it sped up, but not to the point where you couldn't understand what I was saying. It just sounded like Alvin and the Chipmunks were doing the investigation. I wanted to see if these recorders had been damaged, so I put in new tape (by Sony the same type of tape I used for this investigation) to see if the problem continued. I taped for over 15 minutes and they both worked fine. There was no wobbling and neither one sped up and distorted our voices. So I can't figure this one out. I was very disappointed to have missed out on getting voices at this location. Many times, when investigating a noted haunted location, equipment will malfunction for no apparent reason.

When I began my dowsing I was led upstairs into the bedroom where some of the apparitions were seen. Please remember that I was not given this information until after I dowsed. I picked up a male ghost that lived around the Civil War period. He claimed to be around 55 years old and died later of wounds he had received as a result of the war. He was treated there when the building was a hospital for wounded soldiers. At first I thought I was given the wrong information about his age because I was thinking that soldiers were young men from about 18 to 25, but later found out that there were older men who fought in the Civil War. I also found out that a ghost, which has been seen in this house before, has a long white beard and is dressed in Civil War clothing. When one of the former owners came home one night, she was shocked to find patches of white hair all over the floor and sofa. She checked to make sure the hair was not stuffing from a chair or couch. It was white hair and she found enough to make quite a big ball by the time she had collected it all together.

Then I picked up another ghost and this one kept making my rod point to one of my Ghost Chasers International members, Bill Bailey. I asked Bill to give me some questions to ask, since the ghost seemed to be interested in him. He asked if he was a salesman and I got a "yes." Bill continued to ask questions about his age and death and the answers confirmed a story that Bill had read about a man being killed at the Ditto House. At one time this building had been a speakeasy for the neighborhood and one night a salesman had come to drink and play cards. During the game he was caught cheating so he was killed and his body was thrown into the Ohio River, which was just a few yards from the house. This story did not make it into any of the ghost stories of the place, but it is part of the history of the house.

Submitted by Lori Baker:

Patti began dowsing in the back room. During this time, the rods rested on Bill. Patti asked him what he was thinking and

Bill said that he was thinking of a male presence. Through the session, we learned that it was a male presence. Here is the order in which the information was gathered:

Between 20 and 25 ghosts
Some were happy, some were not
The age of the presence was between 50 and 60
He was married
His spouse was not with him
He had between 5 and 10 children; none were with him
The spirits/ghosts there were kind
He was planning on staying
He passed between 150 and 160 years ago
There were Civil War ghosts there
There were female and children ghosts there
He was murdered
He was a salesman
He likes the family that is moving in
He is happy that the house will no longer be empty

After a group discussion, we believe that Patti contacted two entities. One was a soldier and another was the salesman who had been killed during a card game in the house.

Submitted by Pat Crowe:

During Patti's dowsing, I was standing behind Carrie Galloway, who was part of Keith Age's group. Carrie was videotaping the session and we witnessed numerous orbs floating across her display on the video camera. There seemed to be no movement of orbs while Patti was actually asking the question, but as soon as the rods would respond to the question the orbs would appear on the camera display. Carrie commented that the orbs may be dust floating in the air, but I found it awfully odd that they would appear after each question and disappear while the questions were being asked. I felt there was some sort of pattern to the session.

Collected Evidence:
Photos:

1) 30 orbs in a collection of digital photos from Pat Crowe that involved most of the house. A good percent of the orbs were found in the downstairs room across from the stairs. Other members captured orbs with their digital and 35 mm cameras.

Videos:

The Sony Nightshot picked up several orbs on the staircase landing. Also, a brilliant round light that appeared for a split second on Bill's leg during Patti's dowsing in the upstairs bedroom was a great capture.

Audio Recordings:
The audiotapes malfunctioned and I was unable to get any "A" or "B" EVPs. I did however, get a few "C" EVPs that were slight whispers

1) "Help me"
2) "Help please"
3) "Howley"
4) A whisper (can't make out what is being said)

Comments:

After we got home and viewed the film from the nightshot video, I was excited to see that we had gotten several moving objects that confirmed spirit orbs in the same areas where I dowsed. As I was asking questions of the Civil War soldier we got a wonderful bright light that flashed on Bill's leg. The spirit was very attracted to Bill and I think that is why we were lucky enough to get this footage. While Steve was recording with his nightshot video camera, he got an orb during Chuck's dowsing session. As he stood behind Chuck he filmed an orb coming up on Chuck's back doing a couple of loop-de-loops and then going off the shoulder onto the wall where it split and went in two different directions.

The next week Steve and his family joined our Ghost Chasers International meeting covering the Ditto House ghost hunt. He brought his video with the clip of an orb following Chuck and circling around him before splitting off into two different orbs. The camera he used was a Sony HI8 CCD TRV99; it was in standard play mode, with Sony HI8 120 tape (HMP Metal Particle).

All in all, it was a very successful investigation and we hope to return to get more EVPs and other photos. I sent a thank you to Steve and Melody Conley for their kind permission to do this investigation and wish them the best as they try to get this wonderful building back to a bed and breakfast. This will be a super place to visit and sleep with the ghosts.

An orb over the fireplace with Lori Baker, one of my students from Lexington Community College. Photo taken in the living room of the Ditto House during an investigation. We took many pictures in this room and most of them had orbs present. The Trifield Natural EM meter was constantly going off in this room. The photo was taken by Patti Starr.

You can read about this famous haunted location and many more in William Lynwood Montell's book, "Haunted Houses and Family Ghosts of Kentucky," ISBN 0-8131-2227-9.

In the living room of the Ditto House, West Point, Kentucky. Pat Crowe, one of my students from Lexington Community College, found several orbs with her digital camera. I snapped this shot with my 35 mm Polaroid camera and captured two orbs in the same area where Pat was getting her orbs on her digital camera. One is on the door and the other on the wall. We were able to record lots of orbs in this room and several on our Sony nightshot. The photo was taken by Patti Starr.

Chapter 8

Ghost Hunter Tool Kit

"Whatever the scientists may say,
if we take the supernatural out of life,
we leave only the unnatural."
Amelia Barr

The most important things you need to start your investigation are knowledge and an open mind. If you go to the investigation with a negative attitude, don't count on getting good results. On the other hand, you need to be a skeptic, as well. Having an open mind and being a skeptic keeps the event balanced. That might sound like a contradiction but it's not. Go to the investigation believing anything can happen or that nothing at all will happen.

A lot of common devices can be used to assist in paranormal research. Most of what you can use is affordable and easy to adapt for the research. Here are a few basic items you should always have during an investigation. It's a good idea to carry everything in a backpack or tool bag.

Basic Items for a Ghost Hunt (* Advanced, **More Advanced)

1) Notebook and pen for recording notes.
2) Extra batteries (ghosts will have a tendency to put an extra drain on batteries.).

3) Flashlight (sometimes candles can be used, but don't count on them staying lit.)
4) Extra film and cassette tapes.
5) Camera (35 mm gives good results and they provide a negative for proof). Be sure to use several rolls of film. The more shots you take, the better your chances are of getting some type of anomaly in your photo.
6) Recording device with an exterior microphone, or small handheld recorders.
7) Thermometer (to register cold spots). The old-fashioned mercury-filled red line thermometers are very reliable.
8) **Thermal scanners (just point and shot at an area to get a digital reading of the temperature)
9) Compass (Spirits tend to affect a compass, and when present, the needle will quickly rotate or move several degrees on its own.).
10) * Laser pointer (a spirit in an orb or mist form can be seen in the path of the laser beam.).
11) Video camera, (a tripod is better for stationary recording).
12) * Dowsing rods.
13) ** EMF Meter
14) **TriField Natural EM meter (is designed for spirit detection).
15) Ghost catcher - Spirit wind chimes.
16) Walkie-talkies or headset communicators, which free up your hands to do other tasks during the investigation.
17) Large spotlights (these are great at night when you are trying to put away equipment).
18) First aid kit (in case of a minor injury).
19) Small tool kit for changing batteries and gaining access to the back of a device.
20) Magnifying glass.
21) Cellular phone.

Chapter 9

How To Conduct A Ghost Investigation

"When you have eliminated the impossible, whatever remains, however improbable, must be the truth."

Sir Arthur Conan Doyle

Plan to arrive a little ahead of your scheduled time to give yourself plenty of time to set up all the equipment needed for a complete investigation. It's best to select one room as a base where you can monitor your equipment. Try to pick a neutral area where there is little activity. From here, check out all other rooms and areas that you plan to include in your investigation. During the walk-through, use your video camera to record the areas of interest that you are checking out and possible witnesses who might offer advice as to where the most recent activities are located.

Once this is completed, you might what to check your equipment, load all your film and tapes, and set up your cameras on tripods. Next, take your electromagnetic field (EMF) meter into various areas to see what type of EMF distortions you might pick up. Also, if you have a thermal detector, it would be a good idea to check out the area where you are getting the best readings from the EMF reading to see if the temperature is being affected, as well. If you begin to get some pretty good readings, make sure to note this on your floor plan sketches so you can come back to these places and put out the audio recorders to capture electronic voice phenomena (EVP). While you are in an area where the EMF meter is receiving a high reading, is a good time for the other members of your team to start taking pictures. Always take care that you are note picking up energies from electrical wiring, cables or phone cords.

Have another member of your team sketch out the area in which you will be conducting the investigation. This is a great tool to use when you start to experience or notice any paranormal activity. By marking it on the sketch pad, you will have a better record for later when you write up your report. Have other team members taking snapshots as you do the walk-through and making notes on the reactions of the EMF meter, reading from the thermal detector, and noting any other strange movements by objects, such as lights going on and off, unexplained knocking or door slamming.

If you have ghost catchers, or sometimes called spirit wind chimes, now would be a good time to hang a couple of them in areas that will not be affected by a natural breeze or an air conditioning vent. The ghost catcher is similar to wind chimes, so that when the ghost passes by, the slightest movement will cause a tingling sound to alert you and your team. You can use regular wind chimes; just make sure they are made of the very lightest of material for obvious reasons.

You can make your own ghost catchers, if you prefer. The instructions are simple: Using 8 to 12 very thin strips of 1 inch wide by 8 inches long metal, put a hole in each one. Tie a piece of string in each strip and then tie the other end to a pole so they hang down, with about 6 inches of slack in the string. Do not let the strips touch each other, but be sure they are fairly close together. You might consider painting the ends of the strips with glow-in-the-dark paint so you can see them easily at night. Hang the pole from the ceiling or doorway. Remember, any variation on a wind chime will work.

If you are doing an investigation in a large building, with many members of your team in different places, it's a good idea to have hand-held or headset two-way radios, so you can stay in touch. This will cut down on any confusion as to where the other members are and allows for quick retrieval of needed assistance in case one of the areas being monitored starts showing an increase of activity.

Procedures to Execute a Ghost Hunt

1) Interview the people who have knowledge of the possible-haunting.
2) Go to the courthouse and research as many of the previous property owners as you can.
3) Use the library to research news items that would relate to the paranormal activity such as crime, suicide, battles, etc.
4) Get permission from owners to conduct the investigation.
5) Prior to the investigation, take a site survey to determine any natural causes. This could include nearby constru cion, road hammer-jacking activity, quarry blasting, or an airport. Be sure to check the exterior of the house for broken windows, rodents, and tree branches resting on the roof or touching any other parts of the house.
6) Notify the local police department of what, when, and where you will be and that you have permission to be there.
7) When you get to the site, keep an open mind, but use logic to find probable cause.
8) Set up your equipment, cameras, devices, and instruments. Get test readings to make sure all of them are in working order.
9) Document everything to include date, time, and occur rence. Complete your investigation form, which will include more detailed data.
10) Be very respectful of the ghosts and always ask permission to record or photograph them.
11) Be sure to leave the investigative site clean and without upset or damage.

To maintain credibility as a ghost hunter do not make any claims you cannot back up. We all work very hard in this field and we must take responsibility for our actions, because what you do reflects on all paranormal investigators.

Finding Ghosts with Modest Tools

The name of my organization is Ghost Chasers International and we are a determined group of investigators with the goal of proving that life goes on even after death. We set out to investigate and document paranormal activity such as ghosts, poltergeists, EVPs, hauntings, apparitions, and other paranormal events. We have had great success with our investigations. Our findings include anomalies in our pictures, moving orbs in our videos, and voices on our recorders captured during dowsing. We set up equipment and devices that we monitor during our investigations to record any changes in temperature and disturbances in the electric and magnetic fields.

We are always glad to get a call to go and check someone's residence, or a historical building to record proof that there is paranormal activity. Back in October of 2000 we got such a call. We were told that the home of Susan and Ernie Powell had been a quiet place for the last six or seven years, until some renovations took place about a year ago. Susan told of fans in each of the rooms going on and then turning themselves off. She had this checked out by an electrician, but he could not find anything to cause this. She would put a book away in the bookcase and come back to see it pulled out of place. She would replace it and come back later to see it pulled out again. Around 3 o'clock in the morning a great crash startled them out of their bed. They found the closet door, located high towards the ceiling, opened and a stack of books scattered all over the floor.

Susan began to notice that certain objects were being moved around without anyone else in the house touching them and she was having difficulty finding some of these items later. During the investigation she showed me the notes she started leaving on her bulletin board, asking the ghosts to please return these lost items.

Within a few days after talking with Susan and Ernie a newspaper reporter, Stacey Manning, from the *Kentucky Standard*, called and said she wanted to do a ghost article and asked permission to accompany us on the investigation. I told Stacey that she was welcome to join us but I could not guarantee that the ghost would perform while we were there. She agreed that the story alone would be worth her time, so we set a date.

One Wednesday night around 8 o'clock at Susan and Ernie's home, Chuck Starr, Gary Gowen, Melody Schmidt, Doug Schmidt, Stacey Manning, Susan Powell, Ernie Powell and I, sat around in a circle and held hands as we respectfully asked the spirits for their permission to communicate with them. We asked them to allow us to photograph and record their presence. I also explained to the residents and our group that we were not there to make fun of the ghosts, spirits, and entities, but only wanted to prove that they existed. Then in a moment of silence we said a prayer of protection for our group. Once this mood was set, our investigative team began setting up our modest equipment, which included two mini cassette tape recorders, one full tape recorder, two compasses, 35 mm cameras, laser pointer, digital thermometers and dowsing rods.

We placed a recorder in the master bedroom and one in the guest bedroom, where a psychic, who visited the house a couple of weeks prior to our investigation, said she thought there had been a fire because of the heat she felt. This was one of the rooms where we put the thermometer along with the recorder. We checked the thermometer throughout the investigation and the guest room ran about eight degrees warmer than the rest of the rooms. We loaded our cameras, which included three different 35 mm cameras, with different speeds of film (200,400 and 800) and a professional digital camera that Stacey brought along for her feature story.

I started the investigation by using the dowsing rods in the guest room. I asked the questions, "Where are the spirits?" "Show me the spirits," and walked in the direction that the rods pointed. They led me to the same section of the house five times. The rods crossed each time indicating this was where the spirits were. Once the rods cross I have the other team members take snapshots in hopes that we will get an anomaly on film. While in this area with crossed rods I asked, "How many ghosts are there?" Then I asked, "Is there one ghost?" "Are there two ghosts?" Each time I pause to give the rods time to respond. If the rods drop at the number I'm asking that is the number of ghosts present at that time. The rods responded to the number of five ghosts. When the film was developed we saw a couple

Melody Schmidt, a member of Ghost Chasers International, was holding the rods as they crossed in this section of the back yard at Ernie and Susan Powell's home, in Bardstown, Kentucky. She could feel the vibrations of the rods and the energy going through her body as the reporter, Stacey Manning from the *Kentucky Standard*, took her picture to see if she might get something with her 35 mm camera. Stacey had other photographers look at her photo and they offered no explanation as to what she had captured on film.

of orbs in the master bedroom and a small glowing amber anomaly over the dowsing rods held by Gary Gowen.

As the other members of the group continued to check equipment and take pictures inside, I decided to go outside into the back yard with the rods to see what I could find. The vibrations of the rods felt stronger in my hands than they did when I was inside the house. They led me to the same place in the yard three times and each time the rods crossed. The results were so strong and the energy I felt was incredible. From my ankles to the top of my head I was one big goose bump and the rods were vibrating, causing my hands to feel hot. I told Stacey and she immediately lifted her digital camera to snap a shot and the LCD screen on the camera shut off. Adjusting the buttons, she turned the camera back on. The battery indicator showed that the camera was charged and ready to go. When she tried again to snap a picture, the camera shut off again. When she checked the battery that was fully charged only moments ago, it was now registering as a drained battery. Like all good reporters she had two cameras so she picked up the second one to shoot quickly so as not to lose this eventful moment and the camera refused to focus. She continued to adjust the settings and after several attempts was still unable to snap a few frames. While Stacey went back inside to return with her 35 mm camera, I was asking the questions of how many ghosts were there and my dowsing rods indicated a "yes" on the number five.

I moved away from the spot and thought it would be a good

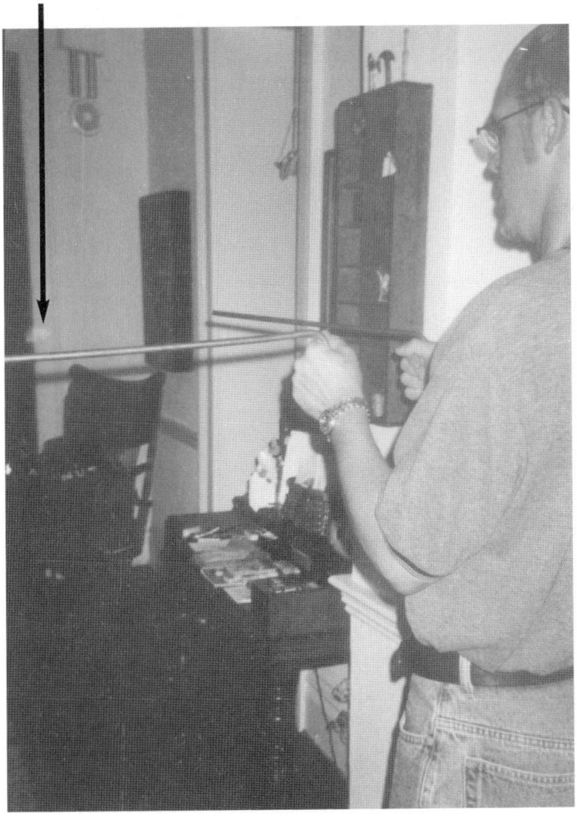

Gary Gowen, a member of Ghost Chasers International, tried his hand at dowsing and Melody Schmidt took a picture and was able to pick up a small bright anomaly over the top of the rods. He was just outside the main bedroom in Susan and Ernie Powell's home, in Bardstown, Kentucky.

idea to see if anyone else would be led to the hot spot with the dowsing rods. I wanted to make sure that I wasn't the only one who would find this area, so I called Melody, one of our team members, out of the house and started teaching her how to use the dowsing rods. I showed her how to hold them and feel their pull. I asked her to walk around in the back yard and ask for the spirits. She wasn't sure of herself but decided to give it a try. Melody ended up in exactly in the same spot where I had been drawn by the rods, and again they crossed in the same place. Melody had no idea that the rods had led me to the same spot. Melody's eyes became big with excitement when she watched the rods cross. She began telling me how she felt. She said she could feel the energy going all through her body. This time as Stacey was returning with a 35 mm camera she was able to get off a few shots without any problems with her camera. Later, Melody told me that at one point she was almost ready to throw the dowsing rods down and run inside the house. I was on the sidelines trying to make her feel better by saying, "Mel, doesn't it feel great? Isn't it wonderful?" My coaching her to hold on to the rods was the only thing that kept Melody standing there while Stacey shot her pictures for her article.

The next morning Stacey called me so excited about what she had captured on her 35 mm camera's film while Melody was holding the crossed rods. There were two flaming balls of fire-shaped anomalies, one above the rods and one below the rods. There was also a green aura around Melody's face and hands. Stacey showed her picture to several of the staff photographers and they couldn't explain the anomalies. They were all amazed!

That afternoon when I got my processed film back, I, too, had an anomaly just over Melody's head in the shape of a milky white transparent shield. We both had picked up strange anomalies when snapping our shots at the same time with two different 35 mm cameras. This made our quest worth the time, energy and effort we took to prove this paranormal activity exists.

Needless to say, we made the front page of the *Kentucky Standard's* Friday newspaper with three colored pictures and a wonderful article written by Stacey Manning. You can read this article and see the picture of the flaming anomalies and you might be able to see the green aura around Melody's hands and face when you visit www.pattiacord.com Ghost Chasers International's website. I was so grateful that the ghost cooperated and allowed us to get the results we needed to show that paranormal activity was happening in the Powells' home. Susan was relieved to know that she was not going crazy and as long as the ghosts were friendly she was okay with that situation. I noticed that the Powells lived just across the street from a funeral home. I told them that sometimes a spirit will wait until after the funeral services are completed before they move on. Because their house had been so beautifully re-done I told them they might experience a visit from a spirit or two, as they wait for their funerals to pass. Ernie made all of us laugh when he responded, "Great, now I have a bed and breakfast for ghosts!"

Chapter 10

Protocol For a Super Investigation

"We shall see but a little way if we require to understand what we can see."
Henry David Thoreau

During any investigation it is important to maintain professionalism through correct standards and protocols. They will help to ensure the safeguards and precautions needed during an investigation. Following these precautions will help eliminate a good percentage of the problems associated with faulty photos.

No smoking should be allowed on the site during an investigation. Smoke could easily be mistaken for ectoplasmic mist. There should be no drinking of alcohol during the investigation for many obvious reasons and because it is very unprofessional.

Check out the weather and if there is fog, misty rain, hard rain, or it is snowing, do not take pictures. If it is cold, be sure to hold your breath before you snap your picture. This will ensure that the mist in your photo is not your own breath. If you are in a dusty area, avoid kicking up the dust as you take pictures. All of these elements may show up on your film and mimic ghostly anomalies, when they are nothing more than the results of the environment.

The camera strap can also be a problem if it is not pulled out of the way or taken off your camera. Sometimes when you are fortunate enough to get a wondrous vortex in your photo, skeptics claim it is nothing more than a camera strap. That's why you should be sure to hold it back or take it off the camera.

Also, when shooting your camera into the sun, mirror, or a lamp, you may get lens flare and that will look like an orb. Make sure to note any other type of lighting in the background, so that when you get your prints back you will know whether the bright orbs are real or merely the streetlights.

It is always good to remember that having fun and a good time while on a ghost hunt is okay. You can talk and laugh, but do not joke or make fun of the ghosts. It could come back to haunt you later (maybe that's where this cliché came from).

List of Standards and Protocols

1) Conduct yourself in a professional manner during the ghost hunt.
2) It is important to have a positive attitude and an open mind to ensure success.
3) Be sure to ask the spirits' permission to record them and take their pictures.
4) Show reverence to the ghosts, gravesites, and battlefields.
5) Never trespass and always get permission before going on the property.
6) No smoking or drinking of alcohol during the investigation.
7) Wrap the camera strap around your hand or remove it, so it doesn't get in front of the lens.
8) Be sure to clean the lens before taking your pictures.
9) Do not take pictures during the rain, snow, and fog, or windy or dusty conditions.
10) Keep fingers and long hair from getting in the way of the lens.
11) Avoid shooting into the sun or at reflective objects with a flash.

12) Be careful of foreign objects leaning into your space as you snap your picture.
13) New tapes should always be used during every EVP recording.
14) Check your negatives to make sure that the anomaly your photo is also on the negative for confirmation.
15) For best results during an investigation, follow the lunar cycle. There is apt to be more paranormal activity three days before a full moon, night of the full moon, and three days after the full moon.
16) Never litter, and always pick up trash and wipe off any headstones that might be covered in leaves. Always leave the cemetery cleaner than it was when you entered.
17) Have at least one partner go with you on a ghost hunt. This will provide more safety and a witness to any strange events that might occur.
18) Make sure you have some form of ID.
19) Let others know where you are going and how long you will be. If the investigation runs over, be sure to call and explain the situation.
20) If you are planning a nighttime investigation, it is best to go during the day and thoroughly check over the site before returning at night.
21) Avoid wearing perfume, colognes, or aftershave. The scents may create an interference with other investigators. The air needs to be clear in order to detect any strange odors.
22) Carry a notebook to record the dates, time, location, and events.
23) Always take a watch so you can record what time events take place.
24) If you carry a cell phone make sure you have the power off so it won't cause a distrubance in the electro-magnetic field.

Chapter 11

How to Interview a Witness

*"I cannot teach anybody anything,
I can only make them think."*
Socrates

One of the hardest tasks for a ghost hunter is interviewing witnesses. Witnesses are very frightened and sometimes confused when trying to remember the details. When there is more that one witness, it is not unusual to get conflicting stories and inconsistencies. This does not make our job any easier.

It is a real challenge to conduct a comfortable interview with witnesses who have experienced something frightening that they don't understand.

As you begin your questioning, check all details of the account and make sure that all facts are in order. Try to recreate the events by placing the witness or witnesses in the same position they were in when the activity took place. Try to recreate the motion or noise by natural means to rule out normal possibilities. Get as many details as you can early in the investigation, because later on people tend to forget the small details. Sometimes these small details make all the difference in the world.

During the interview, be aware of how the witness is interpreting the experience. Is the witness convinced beforehand the house is definitely haunted? This belief may cloud the issues at hand. This is why it is so important to check into all the details. For instance, this is where the location check from your investigation form comes into play. Know if there is an airport, train tracks, or quarry blasting that may cause things to move around in the house and settle someplace else.

Be very careful not to lead the witness when asking questions about the disturbances. Be patient and let his or her own words describe what happened. If you comment on something you think it might be, the witness may have the power of suggestion planted in his mind. Let a witness know you are concerned, but keep comments about the experience in check until all results from the investigation are in.

Sometimes a witness gets so wrapped up in the experience that the truth may be embellished. When they forget some details, they may tend to fill in and this will make the paranormal start to sound like a Hollywood hit movie. Of course, it can be very exciting to think you have found a haunting and this will bring you notoriety, but be very careful not to be swayed by this type of experience. It could be devastating for your reputation if it turns out to be a hoax. Direct questions about the event are your safest way to proceed.

I am including a "Telephone Witness Questionnaire" to help you with your interview. As you ask these questions, you can put the answers on another sheet to attach to the investigation report. Use your own judgment when asking questions. These are to be used as a guide to assist you in gathering information and all the questions may not be necessary.

Witness Questionnaire

1) What happened to make you believe that you were having a paranormal experience?
2) What were the time of day and the location of your encounter?
3) What was happening to the weather at that time?
4) How many others witnessed this phenomenon and who

were they? Please include their relationships and ages.

5) What exactly did you see at that moment of contact? Did you notice a light, shadow or form? Did you think it was a human or another type of form?
6) What did you hear during this experience? Was it a sound or vibration? Was it loud or quiet? Describe what it sounded like to you.
7) How did this contact make you feel? Did you feel threatened, scared, happy, or okay?
8) Did you notice any kind of odor? Was it strong and recognizable or too weak to tell what it was?
9) What senses did you feel at that moment? Did you feel cold or touched? Did you feel you were being watched? Was your skin feeling tingly and the hair on your body sensitive?
10) Did you notice any objects moving or anything else moving out of the corner of your eyes?
11) Have you had electrical problems with lighting or appliances? Were they located in the same area of the experience?
12) How were you feeling physically and mentally when the experience happened?
13) What were you doing when the disturbances started? Had you been reading or watching TV? Were you involved in some type of hobby?
14) What are your beliefs about the paranormal?
    a) Do you believe in ghosts?
    b) Have you ever gone to a haunted location?
    c) Do you belong to a religious group?
    d) Does your religion agree with the existence of ghosts and the paranormal?
    e) Does your religious group speak in tongues?
    f) Do you believe in angels that communicate with us on earth?
    g) Do the members of your family believe in

ghosts?

h) Have you studied or know anything about ghosts and the paranormal?

i) Where did you gain your knowledge of the paranormal? Books, courses, television, or folklore?

15) Before you moved into this location did you think it was haunted?
16) Have any members of your family passed on recently?
17) Are you or members of your family on any kind of medication?
18) Have you been ill or are you being treated for an illness now?
19) Had you been drinking alcohol when the paranormal experience happened?
20) Do you believe in mind over matter?
21) Do you think that your physical being can improve through positive thought?
22) Do you know what "déjà vu" is and have you experienced it?
23) Have you ever had a premonition come to you in a dream?
24) Have you ever had a near death experience?
25) Do you believe other people when you hear about their paranormal experiences?
26) Do you think it is possible for people to be reincarnated?
27) Have you ever played with or used a Ouija board? If you have, did you do so in this location?
28) Have you ever been involved with witchcraft or "black magic"?
29) Do you believe in UFOs (unidentified flying objects)?
30) How would you describe your overall feeling since this paranormal experience? Are you scared, confused, excited, or interested in learning more?

Clues Revealed on Worksheet

I also use another type of questionnaire, the Investigation Worksheet, that I mail out or e-mail to clients who live out of town. I use this questionnaire to help the client and me to figure out if the situation deserves an investigation in the alleged haunted house or building. Sometimes this survey will give me enough information that a physical investigation may not be necessary and I can help the occupants to understand what is happening. Some will opt to co-exist and are thrilled to have a ghost as a novelty guest in their home.

I'm including an Investigation Worksheet of an actual case where I was able to help the clients with their haunting, without having to do a physical investigation. I've changed the names and address to conceal their identity. As you read over the sheet, you will notice that I have underlined their answers to the questions. My response is in italics. This will give you an idea of the importance of such a questionnaire.

Ghost Chasers International
Investigation Worksheet

Name: Debbie **Date:** 4-11-01
Address: Nashville, TN
Phone #: 555-555-5555 **E-mail:** N/A

Please answer the following questions by underlining your selection or fill in the blanks.

1) What paranormal events have occurred inside your house/building? (Check all that apply or indicate in red.)

- <u>Apparitions/ghosts</u>
- Cold spots/severe temperature changes
- Moving/Disappearing objects

- Inexplicable sounds/voices
- Mysterious lights
- Electrical Disturbances
- Unexplained fires
- Doors/windows mysteriously locking and/or unlocking
- Peculiar animal behaviors
- Unexplained odors/stains
- Others

2) When was the last paranormal occurrence in the house/building?
- 4-08-21

3) How many adults have witnessed at least one of the events?
- 2

**It's better if more than one person witnesses these events because of the credibility issues. It's even better if both witness it together while the activity is happening.*

4) In what room/s did the event/s occur?
- Master bedroom
- Guest bedroom
- Male child's bedroom

**Is this the bedroom where your father stayed before he passed away?*

- Female child's bedroom
- Office room
- Living/family room
- Kitchen
- Dining room
- Hallway
- Stairway

**Hallways and stairways are common places people see ghosts in their homes. These are usually the highest traffic areas and probably because of the energy imprinted in these areas makes it easier for them to make themselves seen.*

- Attic
- Basement
- Storage room
- Wash room
- Master bathroom
- Family bathroom
- Garage
- Porch/balcony/deck
- Garden/yard
- Other

5) In what type of building do you live?

- <u>House</u>

**Sometimes, a home can be visited by many ghosts or spirits. It could be a passing may stay awhile and then leave. Some of our loved ones that pass on will come from time to time for a visit to make sure we are okay or want to join in on a celebration.*

- Apartment
- Trailer
- School dorm
- Other

6) How many floors are there in your house

- <u>2</u>

7) On which floor did the event/s occur?

- <u>2</u>

8) What time of day did the event/s take place?

- <u>After 9:30 p.m</u>

**Try to notice if any activity ever takes place in the afternoon between 2 o'clock and 4 o'clock. Also, if you are awakened during the late night hours, notice the time to see if it falls between 2 o'clock and 4:00 o'clock. Believe it or not, most of the ghostly activity reported is in the afternoon around 2 o'clock and 4 o'clock., but that might be due to the fact that we are asleep at night and more* *is noticed during the day.*

9) In what month did the event/s occur?

• April, January

**Think back to April and January. Did those months have anything in common that was going on in your life? Were you or anyone in your home ill? Did you have a good thing happen to you (a family reunion, party, friends or family come for a visit, a new baby born, etc.)?*

10) Is your house a quarter of a mile from any of these? (Check all that apply)

• A cemetery
• A highway
• Train tracks
• Subway
• River
• Mountains
• High voltage power lines/power pylons/power plant
• Military base
• Airport
• Television/radio tower or station

**Cemeteries, highways, train tracks, and high voltage power lines sometimes make good elements for ghosts to find your house. The power lines can produce the same activity that a ghost might cause and it's not the ghost, but merely a power surge. Sometimes a ghost may just wander into your home and you have mentioned three areas that make this a strong possibility. These types of ghosts are not a threat and most of the time their visits are very short.*

11) Is your house located at the end of a cul-de-sac or dead-end street?

• No

12) Is there a garage attached to your house?

• Yes

13) By what means is your house heated?
  a. All electric
  b. Natural gas

**One of my concerns about gas is that sometimes we might smell something unusual and think it's a ghost, but in fact, we've picked up a whiff of the natural gas.*

  c. Fireplaces
  d. Steam Heat
  e. Other

14) Which direction does your house/building face?
  a. North
  b. South
  c. East
  d. West

15) How long have you been living in this house/building?
  a. 14 years

**In the 14 years that you have lived in this house, is this the first paranormal activity you've noticed?*

16) How old is the house/building you are living in?
  a. 1971

17) Have there been any major renovations and/or repairs to the house/building prior to the paranormal activity?
  a. No

**Have you bought or brought any antiques into your home over the past year? Did you inherit any old jewelry or love letters within the year?*

Enter the history available about the property that is being investigated.

Address: 0000 Country Dr.

Owner's Name: Thomas and Deborah

Resident's Name if different from owner: Same

How many are now living in the house/building? 2

What are the ages of the people living in the house/building?
56 and 48

Are any of the occupants suffering from an illness, handicap, or depression? Yes

If yes explain: Husband (Tom) suffering from depression

**Does the medicine that Tom takes help with his condition and relieve him of his depression? Is he on any type of special diet or special foods? Does he sleep well at night? When he has a bout of depression, does he eat and sleep okay?*

Are any of the occupants taking medication? Yes
If yes, what type of medication: N/A

Write a brief account of the paranormal events that have been witnessed in the house/building:

In 1989 my daughter saw a man standing at the dressing room and bedroom. I had a dog that was killed while with us on vacation. I have heard him outside my bedroom door, and when I open the door nothing is there.

**Our pets will also visit us after they pass over. I feel that since your precious pet was killed on vacation, he wanted to let you know that he found his way back to you before he went on to the other side. He may stay with you awhile before he goes on, depending upon how much you are grieving for him. They sense this and linger until they feel you will be okay if they move on. It is a comfort to know that when your time comes he will be one of the first to greet you! All of our pets will remember us and be there for us when we pass over.*

There seems to always be the sound of someone walking on the second floor of our house from the time we moved in. On the night of 4-8-01 our dog (Morgan) was barking at something at the top of the stairs. My dad passed away 1-6-99 in my house

**Sometimes an animal will sense a presence that we can't see or feel. It could be the presence of the pet that passed on or a confused visitor that is looking for a place to rest while he's on his journey to the other side. Sometimes this will only occur once or twice in a family's home, but it does happen, especially when living close to a cemetery. This is not to say that you should move away or that you will be constantly visited. These are just some theories with all the information that you have provided for me.*

Write any history or folklore about this house/building that might help explain the paranormal activity:

My dad's bedroom was on the first floor, and after his death I moved our 3 cats into his bedroom. It was very strange because the cats didn't want to go into this room for a while after his death. About 6 months after my dad's death we had his bedroom door closed and it flew open on its own.

**A person can return a minute after his passing or 200 years after his passing. It all depends on what it is that they want you to do for them. Sometimes it is just a simple gesture to let you know that there is life after death, that we have nothing to fear and death is not the final chapter.*

From all the information I have, I conclude that you do not have anything to be worried about. If you think your dog has come to visit, talk to him as you would if he had come to your room in life. Reassure him that things are okay. Go with your feelings and listen to these hints or clues that you are receiving. Sometimes we are contacted for a reason or to learn a lesson. Spirits and ghosts are intelligent entities and they know if they were to show themselves to you right up front, you would probably faint dead away. So to avoid this, they send you hints. Music may have a special meaning. Maybe there was a child who lived there before you and at night when she couldn't sleep, she would play her music box over and over. Sometimes when an event happens repeatedly in the same area, it leaves a psychic imprint. It can be a person doing a certain chore over and over and like a rerun in a movie you will see this person after they have passed on in the same location doing the chore. That is not a ghost, but an imprinted image, like a negative. Sometimes we get these happenings confused with an intelligent ghost or spirit.

Now I mentioned ghost or spirit. There is a difference between these entities. A ghost is a person who has died and doesn't know that he has passed on. They are confused and refuse to go into the light. Some of these ghosts, even after realizing that they have passed on, are kept earthbound because a loved one is grieving so hard and they stay behind for them. In some cases, the ghost has unfinished business that he is compelled to complete before going on. Even religion can deter a ghost from going into the light for fear of being judged for their sins. So, they stay earthbound. Most of the time, we can help these ghosts by talking to them and explaining what they need to do. Most will listen and choose to go on and the hauntings go away. Not all decide to go, but they do eventually find their way.

A spirit, on the other hand, is a person who has passed on and has made the transition to the other side. They will occasionally come back to check on a child, a mother, or a friend. Sometimes they are drawn back because of a wonderful celebration. They love to join their families when they come together for joyous events, such as Christmas, births, weddings, graduations, etc. They will usually let you know that they are there through a gentle touch, a tug at your bedcovers, a familiar smell, or if you have a picture or figurine of theirs, they will tend to move it slightly so you will notice that it is out of place. Once you realize that you are being visited by a loving spirit and you have figured out who it is, just let them know that you still think of them and love them. Thank them for the visit. These types of visits never last for long.

Unfortunately, Hollywood has the world thinking that ghosts, spirits, paranormal activity, supernatural events, etc., are wicked demons that have come to devour our souls and torment our lives into a hellish nightmare. This is so far from the truth! But kind, loving ghosts and spirits do not make any money for the film industries. If you think about your own life, how many evil, demonic people do you have in your environment? Not any, I would suppose. That's not to say that you don't know some spiteful, unhappy, crabby, mean person here or there, but that does not put them in the evil or demonic category. That's why it makes no sense at all to say that ghosts are evil, demonic entities out to ravish our souls to hell. Most of all, the ghosts, spirits, and paranormal activity are coming from a much more peaceful existence. Once you understand what is going on and you hear a bump or a door open, you can smile and go back to sleep knowing that it's just a visitor from another dimension coming to say hello. This fear does not cease overnight, but the fear level is lowered quite a bit. I still get cold chills and sometimes feel that I'll jump out of my skin. But then I tell myself that it can't hurt me and might need my help, so I feel lots better.

I hope that this has been some help for you and I'm going to send you a prayer that you might try:

Dear God,

Encircle me with a white light of God-Centeredness, a purple light of spirituality, and a silver light of higher consciousness. Bond my intellect to my emotions. Release all negativity within and keep all negativity from entering.

These things I ask in God's name. Amen.

**To cleanse your house if the disturbances continue and you would rather it stop, try this and let me know how it works for you.*

To cleanse negative spirits or imprints

Ancient rituals sacred to any religion are powerful because they carry the sanctity of the ages with them:

Salt - Ancient symbol of purification
White Candle - Positive spiritual energy
Holy Water - Let water sit in direct sunlight for 3 hours and 3 times during those 3 hours make any sign over it that has spiritual meaning and power for you.

At any trinity hour, 3, 6, 9, or 12 o'clock, with a white candle in hand, spread salt around the outside of the house until it's completely encircled. At the windows and doors, sprinkle holy water, making any sign or carrying a symbol.

Go inside from room to room, still carrying the candle. Bless each room with the holy water and the symbol, repeating the following prayer from one end of the house to the other.

Prayer:

"Beloved Father, cleanse and purify this room with the white light of the Holy Spirit. Purge all negativity from within and fill it with your loving grace." Amen.

**When we speak of negative spirits, this again doesn't mean evil or demonic. It could be an angry spirit, a frightened spirit that is noisy, or a resentful spirit that was killed and wants payback. They can become annoying and that's why we use this type of cleansing. By your report, I do not think this is your case.*

Let me know how things work out for you and if I can be of further service. I will send you a prayer that all goes well.

Chapter 12

Researching Haunted History

"There are more things in heaven and earth, Horatio, than are dreamt of in your philosophy."
William Shakespeare

History and ghosts go hand in hand. As I began researching old buildings to find the source of their hauntings, I learned so much history about the sites. I always thought I would be a good lawyer because I love to do research in order to find the hows and whys of a case. While practicing at being a ghost hunter, you become an historian, detective, researcher, and many things more as you try to find answers to these mysterious paranormal events going on all around us. This process will open your mind to physics, psychology, lunar cycles, electromagnetic fields, mythology, dowsing, meditation, photography, sleep paralysis, outer space weather, reverse speech, psychics, channeling, ESP (extrasensory perception), near-death experiences, astral travel, auras, chakras, and more. For this, I am grateful.

Research History of a House or Building

1) The quickest way to find out about a house or building is to ask the residents or occupants if they know anything that

can help you with your research.
2) Another good source would be the neighboring homes or someone who has lived a long time in the general locale and would know of any tales that might help with our investigation.
3) The town library usually will have an archive where you can look up newsworthy events that might lead you to a story that you could use as part of your research.
4) Check the local newspaper to see if you can read back copies or microfilm to look for articles about the area that you are investigating.
5) Another way to find information is to see if the town has a city directory. You can find out who has lived there, how long they lived there, and who is there now. Once you have this information, you can send letters asking them if they know of any strange occurrences that have happened while they have lived in the building. They may or may not respond to your request, but it is still worth the try.
5) Checking with a local genealogical society or historical society is another great way to find out about the people and events that happened in the area of investigation. You can also find out who, why, and how they died on the property. I have had very good results talking to folks in the historical societies. They are a special group of dedicated people who wish to pre serve the true sense of history in their towns and they are most likely to have reliable resources.
7) Gather family accounts of actual haunted experiences passed down through the generations. Add these stories to the history of your family's background.

Great-Grandpa's Ghost Story

When I was a little girl, we didn't own a television, so my mother's stories about heroes or fairies or ghosts provided our entertainment. Sometimes it was obvious that the stories were made up to entertain us, but the real ghost stories were my preference. My favorite was about my great-grandpa and his family. They had just moved into this old one-room house with a dirt floor and a loft accessed by a ladder. The room was a combination kitchen, living room, and bedroom with a big stone fireplace in the center of a side wall. The children slept up in the loft, I guess similar to a "Little House on the Prairie." After getting settled in, it was time for everyone to get some sleep, so they all went to bed. Once the kids were settled and quiet, Great-Grandpa lay down himself and turned out the lantern.

Shortly after the light went out everyone heard the sound of a baby crying. It frightened the children so my grandpa lit the lantern to see if he could figure out what was making the crying sound. They were very tired after a long day of moving and needed to get some sleep. As soon as the room lit up from the lantern the crying stopped. So Grandpa just lay in bed for a few moments, so he could hear where the crying was coming from but he never heard it again. He reached and turned the lantern off one more time and no sooner was the light out than the crying started again. Now the children are getting really spooked and so was Grandpa. He lit the lantern again and just as the light lit up the room the crying stopped.

Being a reasonable adult, he knew there had to be a logical explanation for the sound. Maybe there was a cat outside calling for a mate. Sometimes that can sound like a baby crying. It could be that there was a draft coming from the chimney causing a whistling noise that could sound like a baby crying. He got out of bed and started looking for the source of this eerie sound. He went outside to look for a cat but there wasn't a sign of a stray animal that he could see. He noticed that it was a clear night with no breeze to cause sound by blowing through the chimney. To calm the children's fear he made sure that the windows were locked and the door was fastened. He explained to everyone that it had been a long and tiring day and that the emotions were just getting the best of them. He patted the children on the heads and told them to go to sleep, that everything was going to be fine.

Grandpa lay down for the final time and turned out the lantern. As the dark engulfed the room the sound of a baby crying was even more clear and louder. Grandpa had figured out that if he lit the lantern the crying would stop. So he decided to turn the lantern down as low as it would go to keep the baby from crying, so they would be able to fall asleep. This was the solution to their problem and they were able to get a good night's sleep.

The next day was full of chores and finishing up with all that was needed to set up housekeeping. Grandpa still thought about what had happened the night before so he tried to check out as much as he could to find the source of this strange crying sound.

The second night in the house came with the same results as the first night after they had gone to bed. When Grandpa turned out the light the sound of the baby crying was very clear and very sad. The children became incredibly frightened and didn't want to stay in the house. Grandpa lit the lantern and as before, the crying stopped immediately. He calmed the children down and told them that he was going to turn the light off and listen very carefully to the sound so he could make out where it was coming from. He lay back down and turned off the light. As the crying sound started they all listened very quietly so they could figure out this mystery. Grandpa felt that the sound was coming from the fireplace. After listening a while to the crying he decided to light the lantern and leave the light on low so they could all fall asleep.

The next morning Grandpa decided to check around the fireplace to see if he could find a source of the noise. He checked the chimney from the roof all the way down into the living room. He made sure that the flue was operating correctly and wasn't closed with a draft trying to force its way through, causing the noise. He worked at this all day, trying to figure out why the sound was coming from the fireplace, but couldn't find a clue.

The third night proved to be just as frustrating as the first two and the crying continued. This time Grandpa turned the light off and then walked over to the fireplace so he could hear exactly from where in the fireplace the crying was coming. He thought the sound was very strong coming from the hearth. He went back to bed and turned the lantern on low and the crying stopped as usual. The only way they could sleep was to leave the light on low so the baby crying wouldn't keep them awake.

By the next morning Grandpa had more of an idea where the sound was coming from and decided to dig up the hearth to see if he could clear up this mystery. After removing the stones he didn't have to dig too deep before he hit something. It was a small wooden box. Now the family gathered all around, wondering what could possibly be in this box that might have caused such an eerie sound. Grandpa took the box very gently over to the kitchen table and started prying the lid open to see what was inside. Everyone gasped as they peered into the small box to discover the skeleton of a small baby. The whole family clung together and wept at such a pitiful sight.

Who was this baby? How or why did it end up in this box buried in the hearth of the fireplace? Did it die of evil means and was crying out for someone to rescue it? Was it buried alive and the crying was a continuing wailing for someone to free it? Why? Why? Why, was this baby found like this?

My grandfather took the box with the baby and turned it over to the proper authorities. They arranged a burial for the child with my Grandpa's family and a preacher who prayed over the grave. Each child laid a single wildflower on the tiny grave before they headed for home. Everyone remained fairly quiet for the rest of the day.

That night as they were getting ready for bed one of the smaller children wanted to know if they would be able to hear the baby cry again. Grandpa told them that he was sure that the little baby was happy now. They had heard its cries and rescued it from a cruel, dark place and had given it a proper burial in the sun under a spreading oak tree. He reassured them that they would not be hearing the baby cry again. Sure enough, once Grandpa lay down and turned off the light the only sound that was heard was his snoring.

Chapter 13

How I Learned To See Ghosts

"People only see what they are prepared to see."
Ralph Waldo Emerson

People don't always see the world as it really is. Our brain processes the information from our eyes and sends it to our conscious mind so that we can understand what is going on around us. Maybe the brain filters out these strange visions of ghosts in whatever form they may appear, except for times when a spirit somehow slips past the brain's screening process. Another aspect of this quandary is that spirit energy is made up of a different spectrum of light. The human eye has difficulty seeing this spectrum. But a camera can pick it up and then it shows up in our photos. Again, this is a theory. But nonetheless, these spirits appear on videotapes and in our photos as different sources of light. They can take the form of clouds or mist-like shapes in different colors that can appear to be human form; tornado shapes, called vortexes; or anomalies, as well as thin tube-shaped swirls with orbs inside the tube. Some of these shapes can be easily explained as a flash of light bouncing off a reflective surface, a finger or camera strap too close or in front of the lens. The camera lens could have dust on it or the film could have gotten too hot while being stored in a car on a summer's day. The camera could suffer from light leaks. A mist results from a person's breath in cold weather or someone smoking in the group, or a person's hair could be blowing into the path of the lens just before a shot, and the list goes on.

Just because you have a photo that shows a strange anomaly doesn't mean you have a ghost. No individual piece of documentation is proof that it is a spirit. There are other factors involved. Did you put all the evidence together during the investigation to back up the photo? If you are not on an investigation and you got a photo with an unexplained object, can you show what else might have been going on to make this object paranormal? Being a ghost hunter is like being a detective and gathering information at a crime scene. You need more than one piece of evidence to get the complete understanding of what is happening. You need to be thorough, documenting as much as possible and corroborating the evidence, if you want to be taken seriously by our skeptical world.

I'm often asked if I can see ghosts and I say, "Yes, I can." Then the next question is, "Do you have special powers because you can see these ghosts?" I tell them, "No, I do not have special powers, but I do have special interests and the same special God-given gift to see spirits that we all possess." I have taken this special interest of mine to see, hear, and feel ghosts and developed my senses to be more receptive to their kind of presence. My most favored project right now is not only seeing them, but learning to hear them, as well. We all have special gifts that allow us to learn these traits if we are willing to open up and learn. Some of us learn faster than others, but we all possess God-given natural abilities to experience these phenomena.

Let's examine the physical side of our senses. It's common knowledge that we have five senses. Some people believe that we have a sixth sense, although scientists tell us that there are literally dozens of senses. These other senses are referred to as sub-senses. Take the sense of touch. One example of the sub-sense of touch would be to feel something of extreme temperature. This would fall under the sub-sense of touch as being hot or cold, which is different from the senses that tell us if the object is wet or dry, smooth or coarse, hard or soft, flat or round. The sense of sight has sub-senses that identify color, motion, brightness, shapes, and so on. The human mind is capable of processing a wealth of information from the environment by using our senses and sub-senses.

Once I realized that I was able to see moving flashes of objects in the corners of my eyes I felt I could develop my senses and sub-senses to see them better. The ability to detect motion in our peripheral vision is a protective mechanism to heighten our awareness to possible danger. Though your peripheral vision is out of focus while you are looking forward, you are still aware of what scenes and motions are surrounding you. This awareness is what we feel instead of what we see. Then when we become aware of a movement or change in the scenery, we turn quickly to see what is causing the motion and, for a second, we sometimes catch a shape or light that quickly disappears.

I started trying a few different exercises to help me see these unexplained shapes and lights better in my peripheral vision. First, I pointed my right arm and hand straight out in front of me and focused on the end of my finger. As I remained focused straight ahead, I slowly swung my arm out to the side until I couldn't see it in my peripheral vision any longer. Then I did the same with my left arm. As I practiced, I began to notice that I could extend my arm out a little farther before I lost sight of it, allowing me to notice more area in my peripheral vision. But my favorite exercise is to sit and focus straight ahead and then, without moving my eyes to the side, describe as much as I can see to the right in my peripheral vision. If you try this exercise, the vision may not be clear, but you will be amazed at what you can distinguish. Then do this on the left side as well.

There was another thing I noticed while doing this exercise. While I was staring straight ahead and describing the objects in my peripheral vision, I began to notice that I couldn't see what was straight in front of me, even though I was focused straight ahead. My mind's eye was now in control while I was describing the objects to the side of me. It made me think that maybe our mind's eye sees more in our peripheral vision than our visual eyes do.

Now, when I go into a haunted area or start to experience something of a supernatural nature, I start to focus on my peripheral vision. If I see something out of the ordinary, I keep my eyes focused straight ahead and take note of what I see. If it is a shape, I can tell if it is a solid object or transparent. Then I can tell how it is moving and I remain completely still, watching this phantom in my peripheral vision. Once I can tell if it is male, female, child, or just a faint mist, I slowly turn my eyes, instead of jerking my head, and the shape will remain for a few seconds longer. Then I get a good look at the ghost. Once, as I was watching a form in my peripheral vision, I noticed that it was a woman and she was slowly walking towards me. In that time, I could see her full upper form and that she was very gray, as if she were ill. She had a very curious look on her face as she approached me. I was watching television when this spirit entered my room. Making no fast moves because I didn't want her to disappear, I remained still, observing her in my peripheral vision. Then as she started to move in front of me, I adjusted my eyes without turning my head and looked straight at her. She was shocked when she realized that I was looking at her in full view. With a surprised look on her face, she disappeared. It was the clearest image of a ghost that I had ever seen and I think it was possible for me to see her as a result of the exercises I had been perfecting over the last few years.

I think that our senses are possibly connected at a single point within the human psyche to process information about the world around us. As we develop one sense, all of the others will follow and improve, as well. After teaching myself to be able to see and recognize ghosts in my peripheral vision, my hearing abilities increased to where I subconsciously hear the ghosts speak to me while dowsing. While I'm dowsing, I use a mini cassette tape recorder to pick up the EVPs when they answer my yes and no questions. In other words, if I ask a spirit, "Are you the one who is playing the tricks on the employees here?" my dowsing rod responds with the "yes" movement and I say, "sometimes." I don't realize that I had made that comment until I play the tape from the dowsing session. You can hear me ask the question, and you can hear a voice say, "Sometimes." Then right after that you hear me repeat, "Sometimes." I've done this type of thing so much in the last few years and I think it is all a result of my special interest and training that I have developed this skill. I feel very strongly that almost anyone could do this, too.

I Could See Her Ghostly Shape

I've recently remarried a widower and moved into his house. His wife died almost 2 years ago of complications due to a long illness. When I first started dating him I would feel her presence whenever I would visit him in his home. Once I saw a full-bodied apparition of a woman beside the fireplace while Chuck and I were watching TV. When I turned to look at her she jumped back with shock and disappeared. My dogs on other occasions have started barking in the same area of the room where I have seen her and when I have felt her presence.

Once, while entertaining her grown children at a birthday party in Chuck's home, a basket that had been hanging on the wall for eight years fell and hit me in the head. That day we took pictures of the party and I have orbs and shield-shaped anomalies in my photos. We replaced the basket and it has not moved for over a year. Also that same day the family noticed a smell of smoke and we panicked thinking that the children down stairs must have gotten hold of matches and had started a fire. We all raced down stairs only to find them playing a board game. We searched the house over and even checked to see if the clothes dryer had been turned on. We could not find the source of the smell. It lasted off and on for about 10 minutes. The smell of smoke is a common clue that ghosts may be present.

I was given a glass cake plate and cover by my husband's son and new daughter-in-law and I placed it on top of the refrigerator. I was standing in the kitchen one evening talking to my husband, who was sitting at the end of the breakfast counter, when the top of the cake plate came flying across the room, crashing to the floor. We have a carpeted kitchen floor, but that didn't stop it from shattering into a million pieces. I looked up to see if the vibrations of the refrigerator had moved the cake plate too close to the edge, but the base was still in the middle. If the top had been on crookedly and slipped off, it would have landed on the top of the refrigerator and not the floor. We just couldn't make sense of this action.

When I married and moved into his home my husband told me not to ever lock the back door with the lock on the doorknob. He said the key wasn't a good fit and it was difficult to open. He preferred that I lock the door with the deadbolt, instead. To lock the door with the doorknob lock you have to push in the button and then turn it to the right. You can't just push it in and lock. More than one movement on the doorknob has to occur in order to lock this door. Three times we have shut the door and noticed that the lock was on, because we couldn't rotate the doorknob. My husband would remind me not to lock the doorknob and I would defend myself and tell him I was not doing so.

Sometimes I would smell a hair spray that I used years ago and couldn't figure out why I kept smelling it. I asked my husband's daughter what kind of hair spray her mother used and she told me Aqua Net, exactly the one I used and what I smelled.

One evening around 7o'clock, before leaving to visit our good friends, Russ and Pasty Harris, I set my purse on the couch. My husband was reading a book and noticed something move out of the corner of his eye. My purse was upright and a laser pointer that was in the bottom of my purse popped up and out of my purse and landed on the floor several feet from the couch. The laser pointer was in a case that is very difficult to open. The case was open and the laser pointer had landed a few feet from its case. I had my back to the couch and as I turned around all I saw was the pointer landing on the floor. Then a burst of energy went right through me and I had goose bumps all over me with the hair on my entire body standing up on edge. I looked at Chuck and said, "Did you see that?" He just sat there for a few moments with his mouth open in amazement.

Many times the television changes channels on its own. It does not simply jump to the next channel, but will skip to several numbers higher or lower, such as would require you to punch in the number of the station you desired to watch. The CD player has come on and started playing while we were sitting on the couch watching the television. It is not operated by a remote and in order for it to be turned on you must hit a power button and then rotate a knob before it settles on CD. There are too many actions required for these devices to be turned of and off or to change channels by a simple electrical surge.

A couple of times the phone has rung and when I answered, all I could hear was loud static. I hung up before I realized that maybe I should have just listened for a voice or message. I've been

This picture was taken just after I had seen an orb fly through my office and out the window. I set up my TriField Natural EM meter and it was constantly going off indicating a paranormal presence. I took a shot of the area where the meter was going off and got a face in the mat of a picture that was hanging on the wall. This picture was taken in Patti and Chuck Starr's home by Patti Starr.

very successful at getting voice anomalies on my mini recorder and I never thought about trying to record the static (white noise) to see if I could pick up someone or something talking. Now that I'm prepared to do this, I have not received any more of these static calls.

One evening about 10 o'clock, I was talking to Kristen Myers over the phone when the call started to fade in and out. During this period, we both heard other voices coming through but couldn't make out what they were saying. Kristen asked me if I was on a cordless phone and I agreed. She was on a regular phone and couldn't figure out why we were getting this kind of interference. It is more common to get a disruptive call if both parties are on cordless phones. All of a sudden, a man's voice came through loud and clear and said, "She wants me to die and go to Israel," and then it faded out. We both laughed and wondered how someone could die and then go to Israel.

The next morning when I opened the newspaper I was shocked to see a report about a bombing in Israel that killed many people. I immediately called Kristen to see if she had seen the news. We both questioned the possibility of being given a message about this impending disaster. I was grateful that someone else heard the voices, so I could confirm the story through another witness.

Sometimes at night I can see balls of light in our living room while watching TV and in our bedroom after we've been lying down for a while. They are not so bright that they lighten the room but I can see that they are a milky white and move at different speeds. Sometimes they pass by so quickly that I'm not sure of what I saw and other times they hover. Once, while I was working on my computer, an orb passed me and flew around the room and then out a window. I got up immediately and set up my TriField Natural EM meter to see if I could get it to register any disturbances in the static electrical field or the magnetic field. It was going off constantly, so I grabbed my camera and took some pictures of the room. I was pleased when I got the photos back from the processors to find a face of a woman in one of the framed pictures hanging on the wall just over where the TriField meter was going off.

My husband's first wife, Nancy, was a very good mother and housekeeper. The only negative remark my husband has ever made about her was that she was extremely jealous and at times it was very miserable for him. We have gone to her grave and talked very kindly to her, to let her know that I'm not here to take her place and for her not to worry. We have been often to check on her grave and replant some of the flowers. Each time Chuck tells her something about the children and then he says, "We miss you, girl." This sometimes makes tears fill my eyes, as I can feel his pain of loss. My feeling of her tension is less now, but I still feel her around every once in a while. It's most noticeable when her children or grandchildren come to visit. She loved them very much and I think she likes to see them coming back to her home. Whenever the grandchildren come for a visit we talk about their love for their grandma and how much they miss her.

Chapter 14

Dowsing For Ghosts

*"In the field of observation,
chance favors only the prepared minds."*
Louis Pasteur

Dowsing has been used for many centuries by many different cultures. The L-shaped rod is probably the most ancient of all dowsing instruments. The word "dowsing" means to use a rod or pendulum to find something. It was a method used when searching for water and minerals. In our modern day, large oil companies, police forces, mining operations, and farmers employ skilled dowsers. After World War I and during the Vietnam War, dowsers equipped with rods were used to locate booby traps and underground tunnels.

Both animate and inanimate objects have energy fields. Everything that exists in the universe is ultimately pure energy that gives off a vibrational frequency. This would include every particle, thought, word, emotion, object, and experience. When you dowse for a target, you tune into its frequency. The response from the rods means you are reflecting energy back to yourself for interpretation.

Experimentation and research have led us to believe that the dowser responds to electromagnetic fields given off by the object that is sought. I feel that this is why dowsing works so well with the

TriField Natural EM meter. When I'm dowsing with a single rod and asking yes and no questions of the ghost, my EM meter goes off with each response. Once while I was dowsing a spirit that I thought I had lost because my rod remained motionless, I asked the spirit if he was still with us. Just at that time, my EM meter gave off a tremendous signal for a good 45 seconds. As a matter of fact, I was unable to use my EM meter again until I realized that the presence of the young male was so strong that he drained a new 9-volt battery. Later when I played my cassette recorder back to this exact incident, you can hear me ask if he is still with us and just as the meter goes off in the background, you hear a very breathy, "Yes!" With this experiment, I had a positive response from three mediums: a dowsing rod, the TriField Natural EM meter, and audiocassette recorder. All of these instruments were able to pick up the disturbances in the electromagnetic field by translating the frequency of the communication with a ghost in the spirit world that resulted in a voice answering an intelligent question that was captured on audiocassette.

During the time that the EM meter was going off with such a strong signal, I asked the spirit to please give me permission to take his picture. I was hoping he would take some sort of shape so he would show up on my photos while the meter was still going off. I was disappointed that I did not get an anomaly in my photos, but after listening to the audiotape, I found out why. Just as I asked him to take a shape you can hear a male voice speak over mine that says, "Can't really give one." I think it took all the energy he had to answer my question about whether he was still with us, as he gave the "yes" response.

Beginners in anything make a lot of mistakes and dowsing is no different. However, anyone who is sensitive, which includes a large percentage of people, can get a reaction from and learn to use the dowsing rods for finding ghosts. Every dowser has times when he gets some weird responses to questions. This may happen if the dowser is showing off, instead of taking the rods and their power seriously. It could also mean that the user is tired, feeling ill, or uncomfortable about asking the questions. It may occur at other times for no reason at all. When this happens, try another set of rods. I have about 6 sets and I use them for different projects. I never use the same rods that I use to dowse for bodies in a cemetery when dowsing for ghosts. If after trying a different set of rods you are still not getting correct answers, it might be wise not to use the rods for a few days, until whatever universal energy that is affecting them has passed.

To become a good dowser for ghosts you'll need to practice, practice, practice. I started developing my skill by dowsing in cemeteries. I would start out with the L-shaped rods. After getting permission to dowse I would follow the rods lead until they crossed. I would put one rod down and start asking my yes and no questions with one rod in my right hand, pointing straight in front of me. I would learn if the ghost were either a male or female, a child, what age when they died, how long they have been passed and to lead me to their gravestone. When I got to the gravestone my husband would check the information to see if I had been led to the correct stone. We were always thrilled at getting it right most of the time. This was a good practice for me.

During my ghost investigations I begin my dowsing by checking my yes and no responses. Once I understand the signal, I ask permission to dowse. These are the questions that I ask. "May I?" This means, "Do I have permission?" The second question is, "Can I?" This means, "Am I ready?" The third question is, "Should I?" This means, "Is it appropriate?" Then I say my dowsing prayer: "Dear God (or other according to your religion), Please help me to become centered so that I may become a clear channel to your wisdom, in order to raise my consciousness and the consciousness of those who come to me for advice and help. Protect me from all negative forces while I do their work."

When the prayer is finished, I position the rods in my hands and start walking. I follow their lead until the rods cross, signaling me that I can now speak to the ghost or spirit. At this point, I release one of the two rods to start my one-rod communications.

The first question I ask is, "May I please ask questions?" If I get a yes response from this question, I proceed with my first yes or no question. Usually I want to know if I'm speaking with a ghost or spirit. I continue with any other question that I would like to find out about this entity. If I ask the question, "Are you a male?" and I get a no response or no response at all, I ask, "Are you female?" If I get a no response or no response at all, I come to the conclusion that I may be talking to a child who doesn't understand the male/female word. Then I try "Are you a boy?" And if I get a no response, then I ask, "Are you a girl?" Usually after changing my question I can find out if it is a boy or girl.

As I continue, I try to find out how old he or she is and how long ago he passed over. I start out with a question like, "Are you more than 5 years old?" If I get a yes response, I ask, "Are you more than 10 years old?" If I get a no response, I can figure that the child is more than 5, but less than 10 years old. If it is an adult, I start at the age of 20 and work up. I use this same line of questioning when I want to find out how long they have been passed over. Sometimes I find some that passed over for around 150 years.

If I'm asking yes and no questions and the rod swings around and stops to point, I try to figure out what is going on. I ask if the ghost or spirit is trying to give me a message. If the response is "yes," I start to follow the rods to see if they lead me to a clue. Sometimes they may take me to a picture and then I can start asking questions again. At times they lead me to a person standing close by and then I start asking questions about that person.

Occasionally when the rod points away, I have no clue what the message is and I lose the energy and the ghost/spirit will pull back. If the vibrations of the rods become strong again, I ask if I have contacted another ghost/spirit and start all over with the yes and no questions. Sometimes I find out more about the second entity than I did the first. It's almost as though the first one was getting me ready so I would be really tuned in to understand the second one better.

While I was dowsing a bedroom at the Talbott Tavern in Bardstown, KY, my first question after entering the room was, "Are there any ghosts present in this room?" At that moment my single dowsing rod swung and pointed behind me. Shortly after I entered the room, I had placed a mini cassette recorder on a dresser, which was now behind me. I didn't know why the rod did this movement until I returned home and listened to my audiotapes. As I came to the section of the tape where my rods had swung around behind me, you can hear a whisper answer my question about ghosts being in the room. The response was a clear whisper "Behind you." This is when I discovered the real benefit of having a recorder going during a dowsing session. This was just the beginning of the many voices that I've been very fortunate to capture while dowsing-voices that seem to answer my questions or leave messages related to the subject of discussion.

During a session of yes and no questions, I once got a yes response and then a quick no. This continued even after I reworded the question. Then I realized the response might have meant "maybe." Just as in our lives when a question is asked about something or someone and we are not sure, we respond, "maybe." By this I learned a new signal. You will also learn new signals the longer you practice.

The other day I was dowsing near a family cemetery that was over 200 years old. I had picked up a female ghost and during my yes and no session with her, the wind picked up and started to blow against the rod, affecting the movement and making it difficult for me to read her response correctly. Then the rod made a strong turn and faced me into the wind and immediately the swing of the rod was no longer affected by the gusts of the wind. I was impressed by this movement and felt again I was shown the intelligence of the ghosts that we contact. I was able to continue my questions with no further problems.

Another signal I learned was that if both rods start to swing from side to side together it means to go up or to go down from directly where I'm standing. While I was dowsing a cellar lock-up for prisoners, my rods started moving inward to cross and then immediately outward in opposite directions, back and forth with lots of energy flowing through my hands. I later concluded that it was the place where ghosts/spirits could come through or a spot where there was some very heavy residual energy left behind by ghosts/spirits.

When dowsing an area, I found out that my signals were a lot stronger if I was the only one dowsing the area. It seemed that if two or more are dowsing the same area at the same time, only one would be getting any messages. I now insist on having one person dowsing the same area at a time. I'm not sure why this is the case. Maybe the source answering the questions can only come to one and they choose the strongest conductor of the group.

Dowsing is intuition technology. Like most things in the world, it is not 100 percent accurate and like ghost hunting, it is not an exact science. We are dealing with intuition and collective unconscious sending of messages through a human mind.

Holding the Dowsing Rods

The proper way to hold the dowsing rods is to take the L-shape rods by the shorter ends and hold them lightly in your hands with your thumbs bent down across the fingers. Do not place the thumbs over the bent ends of the handles or they will restrict movement of the rods. Do not grip too tightly, but hold them tight enough to keep the rods parallel and loose enough for them to move. To test the yes and no responses, ask the rods to show you the yes position and they should cross each other. When you ask for the no position, they should turn out away from each other. If for some reason you get the opposite response, you must remember the signals have been changed and for this day you will get the rods crossing for no and them pointing away from each other for yes. That's why it is important to do the test response before starting the dowsing.

In our world today, we are basically wired to the left brain for analytical and linear thinking. In fact, this rational side of our brain is over-developed. Businesses and schools rarely try to emphasize the right-brain or creative intuitive abilities. In order to learn dowsing, we have to learn to let go of our left brain and give our right brain permission to bring up the answers.

The practice of meditation is one of the easiest ways to access the right brain. Meditation is a great method of strengthening the intuitive side of the brain, as well. The practice of dowsing will exercise your intuitive thinking and this will cause you to become more aware of the psychic areas of your mind. Dowsing is partly physical, partly mental, and partly something else. It is a multi-level tool. Use it well.

Prepare to Dowse

1) When you start dowsing, make sure you are rested and have a clear mind. It's not a good idea to go dowsing if you are tired, ill or stressed, since this may impair your results. Dowsing uses a lot of energy, so keep the sessions short. Stay positive and wear comfortable clothes, remove all jewelry, watch, metal objects, such as keys and coins to avoid interference. Do not carry a bag or wear a backpack while dowsing. Your goal is relaxed concentration. It's best to avoid interruptions and discourage onlookers if this bothers you.

2) Before starting, you will want to protect your aura and align your balance to prevent other energies form distorting your success. Take a deep breath and imagine the air entering through the crown of the head. As you exhale, visualize a line drawing down through the center of your body to a depth of about 6" below your feet. With a second breath down from the crown, imagine a clear white-violet light filling your aura all around you in every direction. You have now centered and protected yourself.

3) Check your yes and no responses before every dowsing session since these sometimes change. Then ask yourself, "Am I ready to proceed?" If the answer is "no," try again later.

4) Once you have centered yourself, hold the rods in loosely closed fists with thumbs resting outside the fingers. Bend the elbows and keep them close to the trunk of the body. Hold the rods parallel and horizontal (about 8 inches apart from each other) and pointing forward.

5) Walk forward until the rods cross over in an "X" shape or open into a "V" shape. Return to your starting point and repeat the process for confirmation. Then walk past the proven point to see if the rods straighten out. When the rods

are crossed, take pictures or ask questions of the spirit into the recorder.

6) Make sure that you have a cassette recorder and video recorder running during your dowsing question and answer session.

7) After my rods cross, I put one down and use the other rod to start my question and answer session with the ghosts or spirits.

8) Make sure no one else is touching the other rod while you are conducting the single rod question and answer session while dowsing.

Connecting To The Rods

"I, (Your Name), the owner of these dowsing rods, declare that all answers shall be given in the love of truth when using these dowsing rods. I promise to use my dowsing rods only for good."

Connecting To The Universal Law

"I ask the forces for good to guard all my dowsing, to obtain only answers given in love of truth, given from all available sources, and given in terms of the present time and locations that I understand as a human being on this earth."

Connecting To a Higher Self

"Dear God, (or other), please help me to become centered so that I may become a clear channel to your wisdom, in order to raise my consciousness and the consciousness of those who come to me for advice and help. Protect me from all negative forces while I do thy work."

I repeat these three steps while holding my rods in my hands before I start the actual dowsing process. This helps you focus on the task at hand and gives you protection from any negative forces. I find that when I do this ritual before starting, I have greater success with my dowsing results.

Dowsing Proves A Spirit

Chuck and I checked into a 200-year-old bed and breakfast around 2:30 one Thursday afternoon. It had been a while since I had been to this popular haunted abode and I was looking forward to another investigation, to see what new results I would get. After we finished dinner I thought we would start the investigation with a walk-through, but this time I was going to try something different. I decided to carry a mini cassette recorder, a 35 mm camera, a TriField Natural EM meter, and my dowsing rods. I wanted to be more spontaneous during the walk-through. If I had a feeling, I would be prepared to use these different devices right away. I was drawn to the cellar to start the investigation. Little did I know what was in store for me once I got down there. As I tell this story I have omitted the name of the historic establishment and changed the names to protect the individuals' privacy.

On our way through the kitchen we met an employee who offered to take us down into the cellar. As we descended the steps he introduced himself as Eddie and we began a conversation about ghosts. I asked him if he believed in ghosts and he said, "Yes, but I've never had experiences like a lot of the folks here have. When I have an encounter with a ghost it's usually in a dream." He asked me if I believed that ghosts would visit in a dream and give you a message and I told him I did. "Usually when you have a ghost visit you in a dream, the visit will seem too real to be just a dream," I explained. He told me that his twin brother, Freddie, had a good friend who had died and for a while he would dream about him. The most confusing part of Freddie's dreams was that his friend's eye sockets were blackened holes without eyes. Freddie couldn't figure out why he was appearing that way unless it was because he was dead. Eddie told us that in his brother's dream he would ask his friend to get into the car but his friend

This picture was taken before we did the investigation where we dowsed and got a message from the young boy who had worked at the old bed and breakfast. This is a picture of Cheryl Boone and Patti Starr in one of the guest rooms and we were shocked to see the face in the television once we had the film developed. Notice the black sockets where eyes should be. The photo was taken by Chuck Starr.

wouldn't get in because he said, "They won't let me go with you." Even though he couldn't understand why his friend's eyes were blackened out Freddie could still recognize him. One day the mother of the deceased boy heard about Freddie's dream. The twins were constant companions to her son and she tried to stay in touch with them even after his death. As she listened to the details of the dream she was taken back when they told her about the blackened eye sockets. She said, "Oh, goodness, I know why he is seeing him that way. His eyes were the only organs we could donate after the accident." As I listened to this young man's story I had cold chills running all over me when I heard the part about the eyes being donated. I told Eddie I believe that Freddie's friend was letting him know that he was actually visiting him in his dreams and he gave him a clue by appearing without his eyes. There is no way Freddie would have known to

This photo was taken at a later date in the same room where we got the face in the TV at the old bed and breakfast. I was hoping for the face to appear again after asking the ghost to give us permission to take its picture. Instead of a face we got a heavy red mist in the left corner of the photo. This mist was contained in the picture frame and did not bleed out into the negative giving evidence that this was an anomalous shape. This photo was taken by Chuck Starr.

dream about his friend without having eyes, otherwise.

Thanking Eddie for sharing that story, we continued our walk into the belly of the cellar and I started setting up my equipment for the rest of the investigation. Eddie left to go back upstairs to finish his duties, as the dinner hour was getting pretty hectic. I did some dowsing and contacted a female, black lady, and four of her family members were with her. I wanted to ask more questions but she faded out. We got nothing in our photos during this part of the investigation.

As we were gathering our devices to move on, Eddie came back down to the cellar with his girlfriend. He wanted her to meet us and he wanted me to show him how the dowsing rods worked. I gave him a quick lesson and told him that to get yes and no answers I only use one rod. If the answer to the question is no, the rod will move slightly back and forth. If the answer is yes, it will move up and down. When I'm getting ready to receive a ghost/spirit the rod will start to tingle in my hand. Sometimes it will swing all the way to the left or right to let me know that someone is ready.

As I started to demonstrate this, the rod began to tingle and then vibrated more than I was accustomed to. I told Eddie I had picked up someone with a strong presence, and just about that time the rod swung around and I got a feeling that the spirit wanted to know who the girl was. She introduced herself as Kim and then I was prompted to ask her if she worked there and she said "yes." Once the spirit had that information the rod went back to the question position. I asked if it was a male and the response was "yes." I asked him if he had passed for more than five years and the response was "no." Then, as if in a trance, I started spurting out information that was coming into my head. "He's a male, a young male, he worked at this bed and breakfast when he was 17 and he died in a car accident four years ago. Wow, I've never done that before," I said to Eddie as he stood in front of me with this amazed stare on his face. I asked, "Do you know of anyone who fits this information?" He hesitated and said in disbelief, "This is the boy I was telling you about earlier. This is Roger. He was killed in 1997-four years ago. I know he worked here when he was younger and he could have been 17 years old at that time." We checked later and found out that he did work there at the age of 17. We learned that he didn't die in a car accident, but died after being hit by a car. I explained to Eddie it was still an accident and it involved a car, even though he wasn't in the car, it was still a car accident.

I was thrilled that for the first time I had identified a spirit that was giving me information through the rods. Eddie asked me if I could ask other questions to verify if the spirit was really Roger. I had dropped the rod and through my excitement thought I had lost the connection. I held my rod up to try again. At first nothing, but slowly it started to vibrate. The contact came back strong and I let Eddie ask the questions to see if the answers would match. These are questions that I would not know the answers to because I didn't know either one of these people. The answers were coming through correctly and we found out that Roger had moved on into the light. He was no longer a ghost that was earthbound, but now a spirit who came back for a visit. He let us know that he was happy and that there is

The orbs in the hall, just beside the room where reports of a red mist has been seen and the face in the television was taken, were captured on film while the Trifield Natural EM meter was going off. These pictures were taken by Patti Starr.

life after death. He had come back that night because his younger brother had just graduated and he didn't want to miss the happy occasion with his family.

At this point Eddie asked me to take a picture of Roger in hopes that we might get something in the photos. I asked Roger's permission to take his picture and I asked him to please take a shape so we could prove he was with us. To my surprise, my cassette recorder was still on and at this point a voice speaks out over my voice and says, "I can't really give one." Of course I didn't hear that until I played the tape back. It was true though about the photos. I didn't get any pictures of any anomalies that might suggest that he was there, but instead I got a great voice and was so happy for that.

Then I had the idea to test for his presence with the TriField Natural EM meter. As I set it up, we waited for it to register a presence. After a few seconds and nothing happening I asked Roger if he was still with us and just then the meter went off and I got another great voice that responded to my question with a loud breathy, "Yes." Again, we did not hear the voice until we got home and listened to the tape from the mini recorder. The meter continued for a few more seconds and then went dead. The 9-volt battery was drained from the energy of the spirit.

We spent the rest of the evening taking photos, recording on cassettes, using the rods and testing other rooms and the hallways with the EM meters. We got some great pictures of orbs going down the hallway just as the EM meter went off. I did some dowsing in another bedroom and got a voice on the recorder that answered my question. I asked if there were any spirits in this room and I got a whisper that said, "Behind you."

The most important lesson I learned that evening was to always dowse with a tape recorder close by. Now I constantly get recorded voices from the spirits that answer my questions as I dowse. I'm already planning another trip back to this fantastic haunted building to continue our research and investigations into the other side.

Chapter 15

Record Voices From The Other Side

"Then a spirit passed before my face; the hair of my flesh stood up."
Job 4:15

What does EVP mean? It stands for "electronic voice phenomenon." EVP is the recording of a voice on audiotape, when there is no known physical source. You don't need expensive equipment to have success with capturing an EVP on a cassette tape. The easiest way to do this is to turn the recorder on and let it run. You can have success at any time of the day or night. Some feel that night is better because there is less chance of picking up broadcast interference. The voice is not heard during the recording, only when it is played back. The spirit often speaks in short, rhythmic code or using incorrect grammar. Some will sing, whistle, cry, moan, or growl their message. You can also tell if the voice is that of a man, woman, child, or animal.

When you start recording, be sure to keep an open mind and a positive attitude. Avoid doubt, or it will lessen your chances of getting a voice. Decide what questions you want the spirit to answer. Wait a few moments before you ask the next, question to give the spirit time to answer. Sometimes they talk over your voice and it's difficult to understand what they are saying. After you've finished asking questions, you may want to allow the tape to record on until the end. When you play it back and hear something, let others listen before you give them your opinion of what you think you heard. This will avoid power of suggestion and they can have their own opinion of what is being said. Then have each person write down what he thinks he heard and compare the results. You'll be surprised at how many different messages you get. But sometimes if the voice is clear enough, all will agree on one message that was heard.

Thomas Edison was working on a machine to communicate with the dead. The theory he was hoping to prove was that spirits could talk to the living through a recording device. He was also fascinated by spirit photography and thought if spirits could be caught on film, why not electronically? In the October 30, 1920 issue of Scientific American, there was an article about Edison working on a machine to record spirit voices. As Thomas Edison puts it, when working on his own devices for contacting the dead, "I am inclined to believe that our personality hereafter will be able to affect matter. If this reasoning be correct, then, if we can evolve an instrument so delicate as to be affected, or moved, or manipulated by our personality as it survives in the next life, such an instrument, when made available, ought to record something." Later, when he died in 1931, he had not completed his project and left no machine or plans behind. Edison's dream was realized in the latter half of the 20th century and now we may once again enjoy communication with a departed loved one through the simple cassette recorder.

In 1959, Friedrich Jurgenson, a Swedish opera singer, accidentally recorded a male voice as he was recording bird songs in the countryside near his villa. When he played it back, he heard a male voice discussing "nocturnal bird songs" in Norwegian. At first he thought he had just picked up interference from a radio broadcast. He decided to try again to see if the same thing would happen. He was successful and got the voice again and this time it gave Jurgenson personal information about itself. The voice also gave him information on how to record more voices. Jurgenson wrote about his experiments in "Voices from the Universe" in 1964, with a record.

I have been truly blessed with my success at gathering EVPs.

I started out by putting a cassette recorder in the most active spot during an investigation. As my success in capturing these voices improved, I began to use 3 or 4 cassette recorders per investigation. Just a reminder, don't record more than you have time to listen to. Most of the tapes I use were 90 minutes and, believe me, listening to hours of static can become very annoying. At first I put these recorders in areas where the sound would be least disturbed by team members or residents. This way when I recorded a sound I could be pretty sure it did not come from any of us, and the voice was of a paranormal nature.

My first EVP came from an investigation I held at the Talbott Tavern in Bardstown, KY, in March of 1998, only days after a fire severely damaged this 200-year-old historic restaurant and hotel. After the investigation was over and I played back the cassette, to my surprise, I heard a wonderful female voice say, "Welcome to the Talbott. Have a seat and I'll serve you." She said this very fast, with a rhythm and an accent, so it was really difficult to understand what she said. I took it to the radio station and they put it through their computers to slow it down so we could make out what she was saying. Once we realized that she was welcoming us to the Talbott, I knew it must have been Annie Talbott's voice.

In 1886, George Talbott bought the tavern (known as the Newman House then). He soon married Annie Spalding and moved in with his bride. While they lived there, they had twelve children. Only five of the twelve survived and one of the five was a twin. They were plagued with all types of childhood diseases and accidents, so their children died at different ages. In 1912, George died and left Annie and the family to run the business. Shortly after his death, Annie changed the name from the Newman House to the Talbott Hotel and continued running the business until 1916, at which time she sold it to T.D. Beam, Jim Beam's brother. Sometimes I think that if anyone should haunt the tavern it would be the Talbott family.

Now you can see why spending the night in this quaint old hotel might provide an encounter with an ethereal visitor. But why should the Talbott Tavern have so many ghosts? The mere ambiance of the Talbott Tavern, with antique architecture and quaint décor, can set the stage for a spirit to debut. The impressive history and legends that are connected to the Talbott Tavern, as well as its neighbor, The Jailer's Inn, a bed and breakfast that was converted from the Old Nelson County Jail built in 1819, add to the suspense of ghost hunting.

Why so many sightings reported at hotels, inns, and bed and breakfasts? These places, open to the public, have more numerous and varied visitors, with more opportunity for ghostly experience than a private residence or less visited sites. When a guest checks in and retires to his room, he will be there during different ranges or states of mind from alertness through sleep. It's almost certain that sooner or later someone will awaken to an apparition or some other paranormal activity in his room.

Basic Guide to Recording EVPs

Some EVP researchers advise using a full-size tape recorder rather than handheld models. They claim that a mini recorder is okay for interviewing a witness but not good enough for recording EVPs. Personally, I have had good results with both, but I prefer the mini handheld recorder. Of the four recorders that I use, I have a favorite General Electric mini recorder that I purchased at Wal-Mart for around $25. I always tell my students that once they start having success and get good EVP results with a particular type of recorder it's best to stay with the same one. I know it works for me.

When I first started using the cassette recorder to get my EVPs, I used an external, static-free microphone. But I learned soon that I got far more EVPs per investigation by not using the microphone. When I used a microphone, I was lucky to get one to three voices. Now that I'm not using a microphone, I've gotten as many as six to fourteen voices in some investigations of a haunted area.

I always make sure to use brand new, high-quality tapes. I suggest very strongly that you do not reuse your audiocassette tapes. Even if I don't get anything but static and no voices, I still will not use a cassette tape more than once for EVPs. For two reasons. Number one is, if you use a prerecorded tape, the sound could bleed through and you might think you have an EVP, which would be a false assumption. Number two is that I find sometimes I can go back to the tapes that I thought were barren of EVP's and hear a voice that I missed the first time I listened to it. This always amazes me because the voice will be so obvious and I wonder how I could have missed such a prize. I've also learned that the more I replay the EVPs the louder and clearer you can hear and understand them.

While I'm recording for EVPs on an investigation, I ask everyone present to speak in a normal voice and not to whisper. I also take the time to speak into my recorder to explain any other sounds that might be interpreted as paranormal, like me bumping my recorder by mistake, knocking something over, coughing by a team member, birds singing, a train whistle sounding off, or a dog in the area barking. I want to let myself know that when I replay my tapes the sounds I hear are part of the investigation and not coming through from another source. Once, while on an investigation, I got a whining, whimpering sound and then three barking sounds. There were no dogs in this 200-year-old historical building, so I realized that I had picked something up from an unexplained source.

Another EVP method that I've been employing at a few of my investigations is a question session with the ghosts in the room. I form a group of participants to sit around a table quietly as I start to ask a range of questions. I prep the group to be really positive about getting the spirits to communicate with us, so we will all be of one mind. If there is someone negative, I do not ask them to participate. I ask the group not to speak during the questioning session and not to touch the table or create any other foreign sounds that might be interpreted as paranormal, in case the ghosts preferred to tap out a message. I place one cassette recorder at each end of the table and I sit at one end where I will be asking the questions.

Once I turn on the recorder I begin the session by introducing the method of communication and I ask permission of the spirits in the room to please let me record their voices so that I may prove that they exist. I tell them that I'm not going to make fun of them or exploit them. I also explain what the recorders are and that they will not harm the spirits in any way.

After the introduction, I label the communications with a session number. An example of this would be, "This is communication session 112." Then I tell them my name saying, "My name is Patti Starr and I'm president of the Ghost Chasers International." I continue with, "The members present today are Chuck Starr, Ashley Highsmith, Melody Schmidt, Doug Schmidt, Gary Gowen, Serena Lear, Shoshana Gross, and Ginger Gunter." Then I announce the day, date, and time. I name the place and address of the investigation. After this information, I announce, "We will start the questioning session now." After a moment of silence, I say a very simple prayer that might go like this, "God Creator of all, please make this communication possible. Thank you."

I continue with, "Hello, my name is Patti and I know you can hear me, so please answer me. I am testing this method of communication and would like to talk to you." Then I explain to the spirits that I will be asking them questions and I will be listening for 30 to 60 seconds for their replies. I repeat my name, "My name is Patti. What is your name?" Between each question, I wait 30 to 60 seconds, depending upon the expected response to the question. If it is a yes or no question, I wait about 30 seconds. If it is a question that might require a couple of words or a sentence to respond, I will wait about 60 seconds.

I continue with questions that are relevant to the investigation but I only let the session last about 10 minutes. Once I am finished with the questions, I thank the spirits for their cooperation and stop only the cassette recorder closest to me and let the other cassette continue to record. I've found that when you play the first recorder to listen for the EVPs, if the spirits didn't answer you the first time, they will sometimes answer you while the tape is asking the questions during the replay. Then it will show up on the other cassette that was left on to record. This way you have two chances at getting an answer.

What Does an EVP Sound Like?

What exactly will you be listening for when you replay your audiotapes? Well, one thing is for sure, EVPs do not always sound like normal voices with normal speech. Some voices sound like breathy whispers but are clear enough to make out the words or phrases. An EVP will sometimes speak in a straight monotone, while others will speak fast and with a rhythm. I've even heard EVPs that sound more like mechanical robot voices. In some of my more fortunate experiences with getting good EVPs, the voice will even speak over other voices, as they are talking. This makes me think they want to join in on the conversation, but can't get a word in edgewise, so they just start speaking over our voices. I've picked up some EVPs that start speaking while a phone is ringing in the background, as if they are riding on the energy of the ringing sound. At a cemetery, I captured a great voice that started his speech just as a train whistle blew. When I'm listening to the audiocassette tape, I can always tell when I'm about to receive an EVP because the static grows very loud a few seconds before the speech comes through.

Researchers have classified EVPs by the quality of sound ranging from best to worst, often labeling them as class "A," "B," or "C." Class "A" EVPs are voices easily understood by everyone who hears them, with little or no dispute as to the word or message being spoken. They are the loudest voices you'll find on the tape and the most distinct, because none of the vibrations making up the words will fade away. Class "B" voices will fade in and out at certain syllables, called warping, and are lower in volume than class "A," resulting in sounds that are distant and unclear in meaning. In class "B" EVPs, two or more people listening may hear certain words and phrases differently. Class "C" voices suffer from excessive warping and are even more faint than class "B" EVPs. Understanding one word in every dozen or so is a feat. Class "C" voices are the most whisper-like sounds. Once you become more experienced in listening to EVPs and can tell the difference between the types, you can safely skip any class "C" voices and spend most of your time focusing on class "A" and a few class "B" EVPs.

Once you finish recording a session in a haunted building or cemetery, rewind the tape and get ready to listen. When you hear a message, stop the tape and rewind back to the sound and listen again. I found out early on that the more you play the message the louder and clearer it becomes. This is a process that researchers call "developing playbacks." The more you play the EVPs, the better the quality gets.

EVP experimentation requires a lot of listening and patience. After an audio recording is made, you need to listen to the sound track very carefully for any hint of an intelligent sound. Since the recording is often made with background sounds, you'll need to learn to listen "around" the noise and "into" the track to distinguish noise from a voice.

Quick Tips for Recording EVPs.

1) Use a full cassette tape recorder or a mini cassette tape recorder with an internal or external microphone.

2) Once you get to the location where you are going to record, make notes of your surroundings, which include weather conditions and natural sounds (cars, birds, wind, etc.).

3) Use only new, never used, tapes. If you use a tape that has a previous recording, the sound might bleed through the new recording.

4) Once you have the recorder in place, move the external microphone at least 3 feet away. Then record your name, location, date, and time.

5) At this point, you have two ways to record. You can start asking questions with a pause for answers, or you can walk away from the immediate area and let the recorder run. When you speak during a recording, do not whisper. Make sure you speak in a strong voice. A whisper may fool you into thinking it's a spirit.

6) As you finish your recording, be sure to say your name and the time you ended your recording session.

Ghost Voices From The Mansion

We arrived at the Mansion at Marriott Griffin Gate Resort in Lexington, KY just a little past 1 p.m. to meet with David, the restaurant manager. He and Lori, the marketing and sales director, were getting pretty anxious about having a ghost hunt and asked if some of the employees could join us during our investigation. My attitude on this was the more the merrier, especially when it is young adults. They seem to give off lots of energy and we always get good results with a crowd of positive young spectators. A lot of times the ghosts will even interact with someone in the group, as well.

As we gathered our equipment, as always, I went with my gut feeling and decided that we should start on the second floor. To determine where I wanted to set up my video and audio recorders I visited each room and service areas with the Gauss EMF (Electro magnetic field) meter and the TriField Natural EM meter. Judging the results of the meter readings helped me decide which areas we should get the best results with our equipment. According to our investigation plan, while I'm taking the readings, Chuck, my husband, starts to dowse in the rooms where it is quiet, so he can get an idea of what type of energy might be present. Once he gets his information from his yes and no questions, he records his results and keeps them to himself until we can see how compatible we are once I have dowsed the same area. This helps us to confirm our findings.

After locating what I call the "hot spots," meaning where the best readings were received for possible paranormal activity, I started setting up the video and audio recorders. We decided to put the video recorder in the Blue Ashe dining room where I got the highest readings. That was the room the employees called, "Gretta's Room." Gretta is the name the employees affectionately gave to the prankster ghost. I decided to take one of the mini recorders along with me while I dowsed to see if I could get EVPs while asking the yes and no questions during the dowsing.

I started my dowsing in the main hall on the second floor, to see where the rods would lead me. It wasn't long until I started to feel the vibrations and tingling sensations in my hands to let me know that

I was picking up energy. With yes and no questions I was led into Gretta's room. Once my rods crossed I knew that the entity was ready to communicate. My first question was, "Is there a spirit in this room?" and I got a no response that made me laugh. That's like knocking on someone's door and the person inside yelling out, "There's nobody here." Anyway, after I had a good giggle, Chuck came to my rescue and suggested that I ask if it was a ghost. I knew that. I was just taken back at the sense of humor. When I re-phrased my question and asked, "Is there a ghost in this room?" I got a yes response.

After a series of questions with the first female ghost I contacted, I lost her. I then picked up a male ghost who led me out of the room by responded to my yes and no questions. Chuck told me later that his dowsing and mine were very similar in the same room but he was able to hold the female ghost a little longer and he asked her several questions. The first one was, "Are you a spirit?" and the response was "No." So he figured that it was a ghost and when he asked if it was a ghost it answered, "Yes." He asked if it was a female and the answer was "Yes." Chuck's next interest was to find out how long the ghost had been passed over. By the process of yes and no elimination, he was able to determine that the ghost he was communicating with had been passed over more than 100 years, but less than 150. She confirmed she was the ghost Gretta. He asked her if Gretta was her real name and she responded, "No." He asked her if she minded being referred to as Gretta and through a group of yes and no questions the message was that she did not like being called Gretta, but wanted to be called by her real name. She did, however, tell Chuck that she liked the people working there at the Mansion. He also found out that the male ghost in the room was the man that she was in love with while she was alive and that her parents were very much against this love affair. The information that Chuck was able to pick up during his dowsing in this room was similar to the information I got. This is how we confirm the accuracy of our dowsing.

After he led me into the hall I asked the male ghost if he wanted to show me something and he responded "yes." I followed my rod, which led me into Lori's office. Once there I began another set of questions to find out what the ghost wanted to show us. The rod moved and pointed to the monitor on the computer. It held that position until I asked another question. Then it moved and pointed to a calendar. Again, holding that position until I would ask more questions. Unfortunately, I didn't seem to be getting anywhere by trying to find out who he was or what he was trying to show us, so I asked him if the messages had anything to do with Lori and the response was "Yes." We continued trying to put the pieces of the puzzle together with a few more questions, but then the rod became still and I lost contact.

At this point, I reassured Lorie that the ghost that we had contacted has good intentions toward her and is in no way a threat. He will most likely protect her or any other female working there. I felt that he was very sincere in his attempt to make her feel better about working in a haunted building with many different ghosts.

As we were leaving Lori's office and walking back to the second floor hall, one of the employees asked if I would play the tape back to see if I had picked up a voice while in Lori's office, so I agreed. I rewound back only far enough to listen to the questions that I had asked while dowsing in Lori's office. As we listened we heard something just after I asked if this message had anything to do with Lori and we heard a very distinctive male voice whisper, "Secret." Lori and the others in the group gasped in shock and Lori said, "Oh, my God, did you hear that?" Now more people were coming up to join the group and so I played the voice over again. More gasps and nervous laughter came from the growing group of curiosity seekers.

While I was playing the tape for everyone to hear the ghost voice, David, who was working downstairs in the lobby area, interrupted us by yelling at the top of his voice. He had become a little hysterical and was shouting something about the lights going off and on downstairs and said we had better not be messing with him. Just as he hit the landing, about halfway up the stairs, I turned to face the commotion, when I noticed the sconce on the wall. The lights in the sconce blinked on, then off and did this three more times. The sconce was blinking after the lights downstairs had stopped. Also, the lights downstairs were on but the lights and sconce upstairs were not. I can understand how lights that are already on might blink on and off due to outside interference, but how do you explain a light that has no power coming on and off repeatedly. The sconce light switch was turned off.

This was a sure indication to me that the ghosts were validating the fact that they were definitely getting in touch with us. Since I had the only audio device not recording in my hand, I decided to set up a second audio recorder so we wouldn't miss any more possible EVP. I put the first recorder away so not to accidentally record over the voice "Secret." As I was setting up the second recorder we had more people join our group. They wanted a recap of what had just happened and they were curious about the methods we were using to get these results. By now the investigation had pretty much come to a standstill while I answered questions. I find that when we gather in a group and are talking among ourselves about what is going on, the video and audio recorders will continue to pick up the paranormal activity that will show up on the different tapes. The ghosts seem to feed on this type of energy and excitement and they sometimes will actually say things that pertain to what we are be talking about.

We covered several subjects including, how to use the dowsing rods, the ghost of Gretta, to what happened when the lights were blinking on and off. As my devices were recording I continued my conversation in Gretta's dining room while Chuck and another employee sat at a table just outside the room in the hall. During this time the audio recorder picked up several other voices. Some were very clear and made sense, while others couldn't be understood or just didn't make sense.

Before ending the investigation we decided to dowse in the cellar to see if we could pick up anything. With no luck, we decided to return to the second floor and check out Lori's office one more time. I tried the TriField Natural EM meter and got some really strong readings, indicating that there was possibly a ghost present. Lori decided that she wanted to try the dowsing rods. I instructed her on how to use them and what to expect once she picked up an energy. She waited patiently for a few moments and then her eyes grew wide with excitement as the rods began to vibrate in her hands. The rods began to move and they led her in a circular motion, which meant that the ghost was there and ready to communicate. What impressed Lori so much was how strong she could feel the vibrations of the rods. She said she felt a gentle hand on her shoulder that also guided her to walk in the circular motion along with the rods. She was just thrilled to learn about dowsing. Unfortunately, our audiotape had run out of space so we lost the chance to pick up another EVP at this time.

Once I got home and started the long, tedious task of listening to the audiotapes, I found, to my amazement, there were 14 EVP messages. They consisted of male, female, and even a child's voice. Some of the voices were clear, strong, and monotone. Others were more of a whisper and some were just plain garbled and made no sense at all. I tried my best to make out what they were saying and when I couldn't, I just wrote it out phonetically.

As I reviewed the investigation I gathered all the information from what appeared in the audios, videos, and photos. I started listening to the first tape on which we had gotten the whisper of "Secret." I rewound it to the very beginning and discovered that we had gotten our first voice as we were trying to set up the video recorder in Gretta's dining room. According to the tape the electrical outlet in that room was not working, so Chuck asked one of the employees to check the breakers to be sure there was power to the outlet. He came back and said that there was no problem with the breakers and we should have power. Chuck's response was, "The outlet is still not working, so I'll have to use the battery instead." While reviewing the recorded tape during this episode an EVP, in a very strong, clear, monotone voice says, "Get out of here." To tell you the truth, I'm glad that we didn't hear this message while we was still at the Mansion, because I think it would have frightened most of the employees away, including myself.

This message does not mean that the ghost is evil or demonic. It just means that this entity did not want to deal with us that day. My equipment will sometimes frighten them because they do not understand what it will do or if it will harm them. It's kind of funny to think that we can scare them as easily as they can scare us. Before

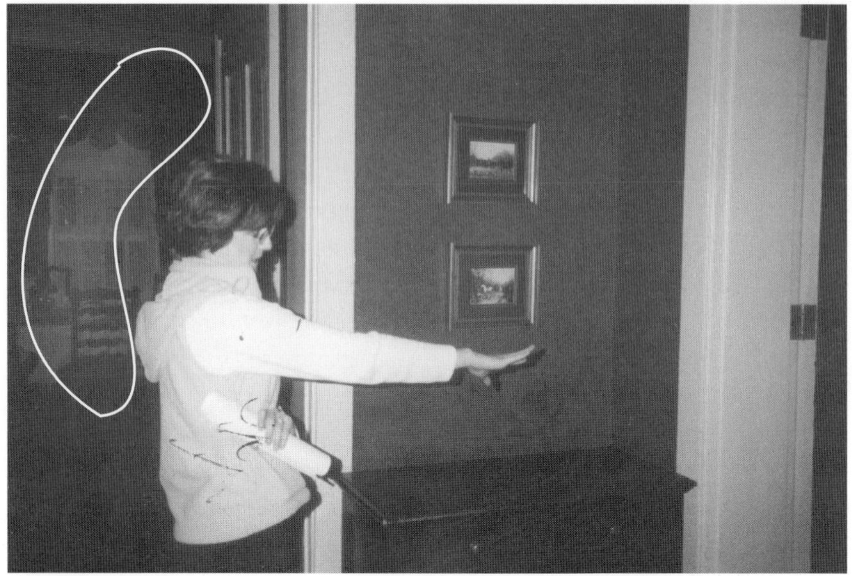

The ghosts at the Mansion at the Marriott at Griffin Gate Resort, in Lexington, Kentucky, seem to love Lori Gambrel, sales coordinator, because we seem to get strange mists and anomalies around Lori while taking pictures of her on our investigations. This photo was taken by Tory Eldridge, one of my students from Lexington Community College.

I start an investigation I try to explain to the ghosts about the devices I'm using so they will not be afraid and will cooperate, so I can record them on video, audio, and photos. After I explain about the devices and equipment, I ask for their permission to record them on film and tape. Sometimes the ghosts seem to understand and I get great results and other times they seem not to trust me and I will not get the good results for which I had hoped. This is why it so difficult to know what method will work each time we go on an investigation. It's really up to the ghosts and they are so varied in personalities, as are we, so you just never know what you might get. It's not difficult to figure out that once we cross over we still maintain the same type of personality that we had when we were alive on earth. The ghost that said, "Get out of here," was doing exactly as I had instructed him to do as I held up my recorder and asked for the ghosts to speak to us or give us a message. Evidently, he was not happy with all the fuss and attention that was being given to him and his message was for us to get out and leave him in peace.

The only other voice I found on this tape was that of the male ghost that spoke while I was dowsing in Lori's office. I had asked him if the message had anything to do with Lori and the response was "yes," on the rod then shortly after that question you hear him say, "Secret." This concluded the EVPs on this audiotape.

The second tape that I listened to was allowed to record to the end and I was fortunate enough to get 12 more EVPs. I had started this recorder shortly after the episode with the blinking lights. As I pressed the record button I asked the ghosts to speak into the recorder and asked if they had a message for us. At this part of the tape you can hear a female voice whisper, "Yes."

Later, while entertaining the other employees by re-playing the ghost voice that said, "Secret," David told us about some computer problems he was having while trying to access a disc. He said he took the disc out and decided to come up and work on Lori's com-

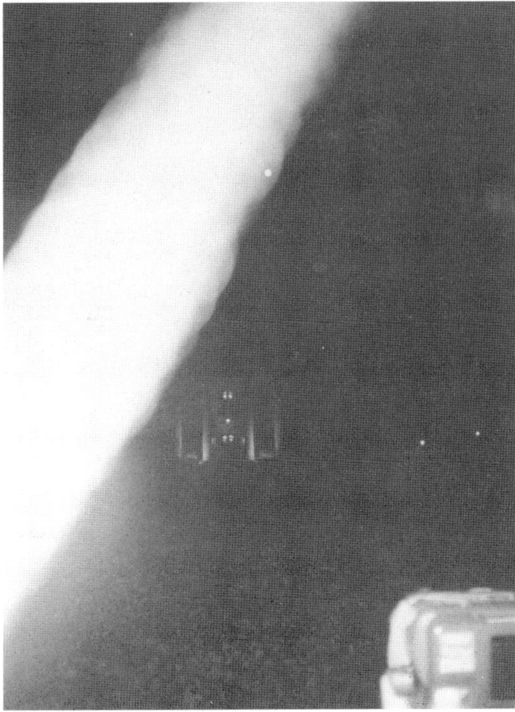

Just before the investigative team went into the Mansion at the Marriott at Griffin Gate Resort, Lexington, Kentucky, Bill Bailey, one of my students from Lexington Community College, took this shot with a 35 mm camera and captured a great vortex.

puter and found us dowsing in her office. We told him about the voice we had gotten while dowsing Lori's office. He figured that the ghost might have been causing the problem on his computer, so he would have to come upstairs. I began to explain to David that I was sure the male ghost was not a threat to Lori and was very chivalrous and wanted to protect her and the other females in the building. Just then, another EVP was heard on the recorder in a whisper that said, "Dave."

While we were talking about the EVP, two more employees, Allison and Pam, joined us. We left the group and walked back to Gretta's dining room and over the next few minutes I answered questions about some of our ghost hunting methods. When they asked me about the dowsing rods, a strong voice said, "Watch."

After showing the employees how the dowsing rods worked we talked about how the lights were going on and off earlier. As we were discussing this event a little girl's voice clearly spoke over our voices and said, "Daddy was causing the lights." She said it in a way that made us think she enjoyed snitching on her daddy.

As we continued our conversation another loud EVP came through and spoke over our voices. The only problem was that the words sort of ran together in a rhythm and I just couldn't understand what he was trying to say. It sounded to me like, "This is my tra ba bay and it will pay low out." It just didn't make any sense. It reminded me of the movie "Nell," about the country girl raised in the hills who developed her own language. It also reminded me of how a deaf person speaks with the sound coming from deep in the throat.

As I continued to listen to the tape I heard a cute female voice say, "You who," as if trying to get our attention. Shortly after that the phone rang and as though riding on the sound of the ring, a strong, clear, monotone voice said, "Devil worker." Then on the second ring he said, in the same way as before, "Jennifer." When the phone rang for the third time he said, "Lady we all know." On the final ring what he said is completely confusing and makes no sense. The words sort of run together and this is what it sounded like, "Running my legs off in here." As I said, this may not be exactly what he said but this was as close as I could make out. You can understand the first three statements clearly but the last one is not clear enough and I don't really know what he was trying to say. This is a common occurrence when you start recording a long message. When an entity is speaking, the longer it speaks the less energy it has and the last things it says will not make sense or be loud enough.

As we were about to end our investigation we decided to go down into the cellar to see if we would have any luck with dowsing or getting more EVPs. As we are going down the stairs a male whisper came through and said, "Hurry." When we got down in the cellar I asked if there was anyone there that would communicate with me, and the rod responded, "yes." I noticed while listening to my tape during this question, I got a whisper, "Yes," confirming the rod response. But shortly after that I felt the rods go limp and realized that I was no longer picking up the ghost. I guess that's why the ghost said, "Hurry," because it was losing its energy to communicate.

We left the cellar and returned to the second floor to pack up our equipment. We went back to Lori's office one more time, but my audiotape had run out of space and we did not get anymore EVPs. However, while she was dowsing we got an interesting photo with ectoplasmic mist around her as the rods were leading her in the circular motion and at the same time she could feel someone's hand on her shoulder.

To our disappointment, we did not get any anomalies in our video. The next time we do an investigation at the Mansion I'm going to take the video with us as we dowse and ask questions to see if this might work better at getting anomalies on film. As I was checking for more anomalies in the photos I found a face of a little girl. It was in a picture hanging on the wall where one of the employees was standing. You can see the face of the little girl just over his shoulder as he stood by the wall where the picture was hanging. When Chuck looked at the picture he thought it was a reflection of my face but I wasn't in that room at the time he took that shot. After looking at the picture with a magnifying glass you can see the face of the little girl in the mat of the picture.

Altogether this was a fantastic investigation and I was extremely pleased with all of our results. This case will definitely help in my

research of ghosts and the paranormal.
To conclude with my results:

1) There were more than 20 but less than 30 ghosts at the time we held the investigation.
2) There were 8 male voices, 3 female voices, and one child's voice.

Here is a list of the voices in the order that they spoke to us:

1) "Get out of here!" very clear and strong.
2) "Secret," a male whisper, protective, different from the first voice.
3) "Yes," a female whisper, friendly.
4) "Dave," a male voice recorded twice in two different areas.
5) "Watch," just after someone asked about dowsing.
6) "Daddy was causing the lights," a little girl happy to snitch on daddy.
7) "This is my try ba bay and it will pay low out," couldn't figure this one out.
8) "You who," young female trying to get our attention.
9) "Devil worker", male and very clear and loud.
10) "Jennifer," same male as above.
11) "Lady we all know," same male as above.
12) "Running my legs off in here," same male as above.
13) "Hurry," a male whisper, sounds like the same male that said "Secret."
14) "Yes," a male whisper.

We got five pictures that have ghostly anomalies:

1) While Lori is dowsing 2 photos of a shape of a man in the flash.
2) Another 2 photos of ectoplasmic mist as Lori is dowsing.
3) A child's face (little girl) in the mat of a hanging picture

with Brandon standing beside it. You can see her just above his shoulder.

The paranormal activity that goes on at the Mansion is the result of many ghosts and they each have their own personality. They are not evil or demonic in any way. As a matter of fact, most of them have a neat sense of humor and displayed this while we were there. Through this investigation and all the information that I was able to gather I can honestly say that they are friendly and loving ghosts. They love the people who work there and find that the guests there are interesting and add variety to their existence. My hope is that everyone will continue to co-exist with respect for all. This is an ideal environment to keep the ghosts of the Mansion happy and safe.

I sent a thank you to the staff at the Mansion for allowing us to complete this investigation in a professional manner with their help. They were quick to lend a hand and whatever we needed they were happy to accommodate. The energy within this spirited staff, no pun intended, was very refreshing and I can see why this establishment is so successful. They carry a sense of pride that exuded in every aspect of what is expected of them. If I were a ghost, the Mansion at the Marriott Griffin Gate Resort would be my first choice to haunt.

Chapter 16

A Terrific Ghost Detector

"Whoever has done good in the main has spirit-energy that is pure and clear when death comes."

Lu Yen

The law of physics states that matter and energy cannot be created or destroyed, only transferred. Water, for example, can exist in three different forms. The first form is a liquid that can be frozen into ice, a solid form, and then heated to create steam, a gaseous form. Since the water still contains the same essence of itself in the other forms, it would only make sense that we also contain the essence of who we are after death. Our energy is not destroyed at death, but transformed into another configuration. The energy is detectable with a TriField Natural EM meter that measures the milligauss units. It was designed to ignore power lines, appliances and other man made EMF sources. The meter measures low static electric, radio-microwave, magnetic fields, and the electrical field carried by humans and animals.

The TriField Natural EM meter is one of the most reliable and most popular devices used by ghost hunters today. This instrument will register when a spirit is near, confirming our instincts in the field. How does it work? It is believed that the energy of a ghost, conscious spirit, or any other paranormal energy causes a disruption in a location's magnetic field. When this energy is present, this measuring device detects them.

When you turn the meter on, the needle will flip back and forth to adjust itself as it returns to 0. There is a whining noise that will alarm when the EM registers around 4 to 100. By turning the knob on the EM meter to "Sum," you get the electromagnetic reading for which you are looking. The range you want to look for is 2 through 7. Usually a reading in that range means detection of paranormal activity.

As you walk about, hold the EM meter in the open palm of your hand. When you start to pick up readings, stop and wait for the meter to balance itself and hone in on the spirit. Once the reading has stabilized, you will know how strong it is. As the meter is registering the entity's presence and the alarm is whining, have someone take pictures all around that area. Again, it's up to the ghosts to cooperate and allow us to capture them on film. The main goal of the investigation is to come away with as much evidence as your devices, instruments, and cameras can record.

It seems that whenever I'm called to investigate a possible ghost haunting or poltergeist, I find certain electrical elements at work. The EM meter measures and records even the smallest fluctuation in the surroundings' electromagnetic field. All objects give off some type of electromagnetic field, even our own bodies. Large electrical appliances will give off higher distortions than smaller ones. When ghosts come into an area, they cause an even higher level of electromagnetic distortion and create high levels of static electricity. These high levels of distortion have been known to affect the working ability of audio and video equipment, and computers, as well.

The TriField ® Natural EM Meter

Before you start using your meter, turn the knob to "Battery Test." The needle should be on or to the right of the diagonal line that is to the right of those words, on the meter scale. If the needle reads left of the line, replace the 9-volt battery by unscrewing the four back screws. A regular 9-volt battery should last for about 10 hours of testing. If you use an alkaline battery, it will last for about 50 hours.

When you place the dial on "Magnetic," the meter will read any changes in the magnetic field caused by rotating the meter in the earth's magnetic field, by a moving magnetic object, or by DC currents carried by wires or the atmosphere. The earth's field strength is about 50 microteslas (500 milligauss), so rotating the meter from north to south rapidly (within a 0.5 second interval) causes a momentary reading of about 100 (a change from -50 to +50). If subsequently held still, the needle will settle back to zero. For the best readings of transient fields, the meter should be placed on a stationary object because of its sensitivity to slight rotations while in your hand.

Though your body produces very little magnetic field, the electric field is strong enough to be measured. Turn the knob to "Electric" and multiply the reading by 10 to get units of V/m (volts per minutes); thus a momentary needle peak at full scale means the field changed by 1000V/m. During a thunderstorm, the electric field will fluctuate indoors by as much as 100 V/m. At other times, the fluctuation is less than 3 V/m, so indoor transient phenomena are easier to detect during calm weather. Set the meter upright on a stationary metal surface for greater sensitivity.

As you turn the dial to "Sum," the meter will add any changes in the electric field to any changes in the magnetic field, so that if either field increases or decreases, the needle will rise above zero.

The "Radio/microwave" setting directly reads radio waves from 100 KHz to 3 GHz, and can detect fairly weak localized radio sources if the top of the meter is held close to the source. In most cases, this always reads zero. It can also check a microwave oven for leakage. If you turn the oven on and stand six feet away, the meter should read less than half scale, or 0.2 milliwatts per square centimeter for a properly functioning oven. If it reads higher than 0.2, have the door seal repaired.

The side knob of the meters controls the tone threshold. The tone sounds only if the needle deflection is sufficiently high. The tone won't sound at all if the knob is turned all the way counterclockwise.

The TriField ® Natural EM meter detects changes in extremely weak static (DC or natural) electric and magnetic fields. It signals with both a tone and the movement of the needle-type gauge if either the electric or magnetic field changes from previous levels. A radio and microwave detector is also included, which reads radio power directly if any transmitters are nearby. Because man-made AC electric and magnetic fields are very common and could interfere with readings of static fields, the meter has been designed to ignore the AC fields of power lines, appliances, and other objects that would emit these frequencies.

The TriField ® Natural EM meter was designed to do field measurements for special research. It can detect geomagnetic storms caused by unusual solar activity interacting with the ionosphere (which results in rapid changes of up to 10 percent in the earth's magnetic field), as well as electrical activity of ordinary thunderstorms. Ball lightning should, in theory, be associated with a strong magnetic field, and magnetization of metal on the ground has been reported with some sightings of unusual lights in the sky. When set on "Magnetic," the meter will signal the movement of any distant, strong magnetic sources in the sky, even if the sky is cloudy or the source dips behind a hill. Because house construction materials generally do not block magnetic fields, the meter can be placed indoors and will work equally well. Because of the built-in tone, it can be used in the dark, and will sound the tone at whatever setting you place the dial.

The meter is sensitive to changes of as little as 0.5 percent of the strength of the earth's magnetic field, and the tone will sound whether the field increases or decreases. After the meter detects an event, when the magnetic field then becomes stable for more than five seconds, the tone will stop and the needle will return to zero. The meter will remain at rest until the field changes [illegible] The threshold level (squelch level) of the tone is adjustable. You can determine the amount of change in the magnetic field required to the tone. If the field changes by the threshold amount, the tone will come on at a low pitch. If the amount of change is larger, the tone's pitch will be higher.

When the dial is set to "Electric," the meter is sensitive to electric fields as weak as 3 V/m. To illustrate just how feeble a field this is, a 10x10x10 foot room filled with a field of this strength has a total amount of energy equivalent to that required to lift a single grain of table salt one fiftyeth of an inch. Indoors, electric fields typically fluctuate 1 or 2 V/m. By setting the minimum sensitivity to change at 3 V/m, we have a meter designed to disregard this "background noise." Human beings and animals usually emit an electric field, which is easily detectable using the TriField Natural EM meter. In fact, the meter can be used as a motion-activated intruder alarm. It is so sensitive that it can detect the presence of a person through a wall. Though it is not foolproof in this capacity, (sometimes a person will carry no electric charge and thus be invisible to the meter), its sensitivity is of interest to researchers in the field of parapsychology. Every type of detectable physical manifestation ("Type of Effect or Field" in the table below) requires a certain amount of energy. For example, moving air requires the expenditure of a small amount of energy initially. Below is a table showing several types of effects or fields emitted by people and objects. It also shows the minimum amount of energy required (per cubic foot of air) to set up that effect or field so it is stronger than typical indoor background noises for that effect or field. Clearly the static electric field is the type that requires the least energy to be detectable.

Type of effect or field	Energy needed (watts-second)	Emitted by people?	Are instruments needed to detect this?
Heat	30	yes	thermal viewer
Moving air	1/10,000	yes	no (can feel this)
Static magnetic	1/20 million	no	magnetic meter
Sound	1/100 million	yes	no
Ligh	1/billion	no	no
Static electric	1/10 billion	yes	electric meter

The radio/microwave detector is sensitive from 100,000 to 2.5 billion oscillations per second (100 KHz to 2.5 GHz) and can detect strong or unusual atmospheric electrical activity. It can also detect leaky microwave ovens, cellular or portable phones, walkie-talkies and concealed surveillance bugs. Its minimum and maximum detectable signal strengths are .01 milliwatt/cm2 and 1 milliwatt/cm2, respectively.

The "Sum" setting adds together the electric and magnetic fields and detects if either field changes. The Natural EM meter is used to find disturbance in either type of field, but in the "Sum" setting it can generally detect if a person approaches to within 5 to 10 feet, even on the other side of a wall. For this reason, the Natural EM meter is preferred for parapsychological research, when for example, a room to be measured is known to be vacant for an extended period, except for experimenters, who remain relatively still for that period.

The Trifield ® Natural EM meter can be purchased through AlphaLab, Inc. at www.trifieldmeter.com.

Chapter 17

Clearing Out The Ghosts

"An Idea, like a ghost...must be spoken to a little before it will explain itself."
Charles Dickens

There is no proof that prayers, clearings, or exorcisms consistently help. In some cases, it might get worse. Before I start a clearing, I like to explain what might be going on to the person or persons who are being affected by the spirit. I don't consider myself a psychic, but I do know that ghosts need to be treated with respect and understanding. Suppose you woke up one day and looked around your house and it didn't look the same? Suppose someone had moved all the furnishings around and you didn't recognize most of the things in your house. Then suppose you found yourself surrounded by a family you had never met. You are really confused and have no idea what is happening. To add injury to insult, someone in the family screams out, "Hey, whoever you are! This is our house now and you are not welcome, so get out!" How would that make you feel? You would probably get very angry and even more confused. Would you get up and leave? I think not. You would probably try to find a way to get rid of the intruders who have rudely taken over your space.

Some of the things I'm about to tell you can and may work for a situation involving the clearing out of a ghost. Just remember, there are no guarantees. This is not an exact science and may or may not work. The results vary from case to case.

Removing the Family Ghost

Stand together as a family, holding hands to form a circle. With a sincere voice, tell the ghost that you have an urgent message for him/her and to listen closely. Tell him that he is no longer a part of the earth plane and needs to continue the journey home. Tell him that that he has friends and family waiting for him and all he has to do is call them to come and assist him into the warm and loving light. Tell him that by going into the light he will find a place where he will be free to make his own home any way his heart desires. He will be met by angels, friends, family, and pets that are anxiously waiting to see him. He has no reason to fear judgment or punishment of any kind. He will only find love and understanding in his new place to live. Then tell him that you are all sending him love and prayers as he moves on his way.

If you are commanding and ask the ghost to get out of your house, you may cause him to react with anger and create a backlash, which means that the ghost could start to increase his activity. If you feel the spirit is negative or a prankster, you can ask firmly, but with respect, that it not scare you or your children.

Rituals to Clear a Ghost

1) Smudging: You can burn sage to help with a clearing. Start at the front door and leave it open. Walk counterclockwise around the inside of the room. When the circle is completed, the spirits can leave through the open front door.

2) Holy water: For this ritual you will need a white candle, salt, and holy water. You can make the holy water yourself by placing water in a container and leaving it out in the sun for 3 hours. During that time, make the sign of the cross over the water three times. Do the ritual at night and use the white candle to light your way as you encircle the house with the salt and sprinkle each window and door

seal with the holy water. After you have completed this, you can say a prayer to clear the house of all negative energies.

3) Professional counseling: Sometimes a spirit is drawn to an individual who might be suffering from depression or other negative emotions buried deep inside. Getting counseling and freeing these negative emotions can sometimes be the key to removing unwanted spirits.

If none of the above seem to help and you are still plagued with the discomforts of an unwanted ghost, you may want to seek a reputable ghost hunter to come in and record the activity. With the investigative report, you will have something to present to a clergyman who might consider exorcism.

Chapter 18

Ouija Board is Not Just a Game

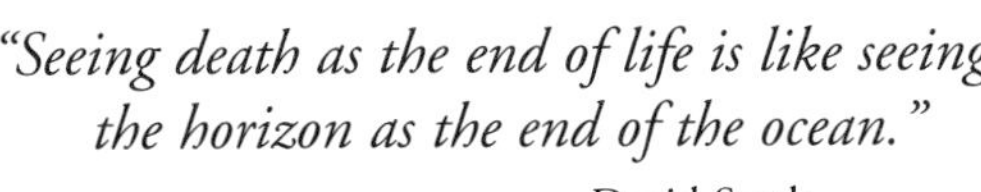

"Seeing death as the end of life is like seeing the horizon as the end of the ocean."

David Searls

In the middle 1800s, with the onset of spiritualism, man's quest was ripe to communicate with the dead. As the great demands for mediums, acting as intermediaries between spirits and humans grew, so did the invention of a variety of interesting ways to communicate with the dead. Out of these different techniques came the most famous method of all, the Ouija board. From this method of communication evolved a more sophisticated instrument called a planchette, a small heart-shaped table with two rotating casters underneath and a pencil at the apex formed by the three legs. It was less noisy than tapping, where the medium and others place their fingers on the table and as the table would tilt over it would tap on the floor in a code for each letter of the alphabet.

Legend has it that the inventor was a French medium, M. Planchette, but there is no information to back this claim. Besides, the word planchette in French means, "little plank." By the end of the 1800s, the planchette was a favorite parlor game sold by many toy companies in the United States and Europe.

Mediums using the table tapping method soon became bored

when the novelty of the tilting table wore off and the task of translating the taps to letters was so time consuming. Even the planchette writing was often arduous and most times hard to read. Before the message was complete, the planchette would slide to another corner and then back again making it difficult to keep it centered long enough to get a complete message. Soon, most mediums stopped using the planchette and opted for going into trances to receive spirit messages. Other mediums, having abandoned the planchette, kept the pencils to write the message, as the spirits would come through them and control their writing. Some of the mediums felt strongly that there should be some sort of device to help them communicate, if they were going to reach the spirit world correctly. All sorts of interesting new alphanumeric contraptions were showing up along with weird-looking tables and pulley devices that had letters, wheels, and moving needles. Out of these was created the "talking board."

E. C. Reiche, Elijah Bond, and Charles Kennard, together came up with a design for a new board. The letters of the alphabet were spread in twin arcs across the middle of the board. Below the letters were numbers 1 to 10. In the corners were "Yes" and "No." The planchette was changed, as well. The shape was more like a paddle and the coasters were removed and replaced with padded wooden pegs to allow a smooth glide over the face of the board. Once you had contacted the spirit world, the planchette would start to move from letter to letter to spell out its message. It is noted that Kennard named the new board, "Ouija," after an Egyptian word for good luck. There is no Egyptian word for good luck, but the board supposedly instructed him to name it that during a session, so the name remains. Kennard went on to develop the Kennard Novelty Company and in 1890 began producing the first commercial line of Ouija boards. Here is one of his advertisements found in a Hollis Street Theatre program dated November 7, 1891, in Boston, Mass.

OUIJA
A WONDERFUL TALKING BOARD

Interesting and mysterious; surpasses in its results second sight, mind reading, clairvoyance; will give intelligent answer to any question. Proven at patent office before patent was allowed. Price $1.50. All first-class toy, dry goods, and stationary stores. W. S. Carr & Co., 83 Pearl street; New England News Co., 14 Franklin street; H. Partridge & Co., Hanover and Washington streets; R. Schwarz, 458 Washington street: R.H. White & Co.; Houghton & Dutton.

Unfortunately in 1892, a very short time after Kennard started his Ouija business, a hostile takeover by his financial supporters forced him out of the company. William Fuld, Kennard's former shop supervisor, became the new owner. It was Fuld, with fate in control, that history credits as the "Father of the Ouija Board."

The name of the company was changed to Ouija Novelty Company. Along with Fuld's business partner and brother, Isaac, they began to manufacture the Ouija board in record numbers. Fuld went on to become the most successful Ouija board producer of his time. In addition to his toy business, he was also a United States Customs Inspector and a member of Baltimore's General Assembly.

Fuld's first public relations scheme was to rewrite the history of the Ouija board. He claimed to have invented the board and chose the name Ouija from two words—-"oui" meaning "yes" in French, and "ja" for "yes" in German. All of these changes came about in hopes of continuing to boost sales.

For thirty-five years William Fuld ran his firm through hard times and good times. Regrettably, in February of 1927, while he was helping a worker adjust a flagpole that was being replaced on the roof of his factory, the brace he was holding onto gave way and he fell backwards to his death on the street below. Though several witnessed this horrific accident, it was rumored that Fuld was depressed and had actually committed suicide by jumping off the roof.

Fuld's children took over the company and began to develop other entertaining Ouija boards of their own version. After thirty-nine years of success, in 1966, the Fuld brothers retired and sold the company to the Parker Brothers. Today this company owns all the rights and trademarks to the Ouija board and still sells it in large quantities. It continues to produce an accurate Fuld reproduction and even made a deluxe wooden edition of the Ouija board for a brief time. In 1999, Parker Brothers stopped the production of the classic Fuld Ouija board and designed a smaller, less detailed, glow-in-the-dark rendition. Parker Brothers' slogan for the Ouija board is, "It's only a game. Isn't it?"

Even though the Ouija Board is sold as a children's game it should be taken very seriously. The game of contacting spirits lacks safeguards and because of this it is not a good source for determining ghosts and their stories. People who use the game can never be certain what type of spirit they may bring into their space. If at any time the messages become negative or malevolent, stop all communications immediately!

Remember, if you insist on trying a game with the Ouija Board, always begin each session with a prayer. Imagine you, the room, and everything in it enveloped in a bright white light. White is the color that represents goodness and purity. This is a key for opening the spiritual door so you will be protected in case something unpleasant shows up. Use the Ouija Board with trusted friends and never use it as a toy for amusement. Despite the Parker Brother's slogan, the Ouija Board is not just a game.

Chapter 19

Spirit Photography

"One should not stand at the foot of a sick person's bed, because that place is reserved for the guardian angel."

Jewish Folk Saying

Have you ever had pictures developed and as you were checking them out found strange-looking shapes, round objects, a misty cloud, or streaks of light that didn't belong there? Did you think that these anomalies were the fault of the camera, film or the developer, so you took them back for a refund? Maybe the photos were fine and you actually caught a ghost on film in their most common form.

I find that one of the most intriguing aspects of ghost hunting is photography. Ghost photography is the capturing of unexplained natural or supernatural images using a camera and film. The camera becomes a medium between the photographer and subject, which is a form of electronic spirit communication. This link between electromagnetic energies and devices is becoming clearer to those of us who look to communicate with energies identified as spirits. Since I am at a loss as to why, how, and what is happening scientifically, I choose to understand the spiritual aspect of "why."

History of Spirit Photography

Shortly after the birth of modern spiritualism came the practice in 1861 of attempting to capture ghosts on film. William H. Mumler, a Boston engraver, took a picture of himself and claimed he discovered a ghost in the photo with him. Mumler soon figured out that he could probably make a lot of money by arranging for people to come to his studio for "Séance Photography" sessions. He claimed that he had the power to summon up their dead loved ones and have them appear in the photos. It didn't take long for this to catch on and Mumler was making a lot of money taking these séance photos. In 1872 he was exposed in court as a fake.

Early cameras required the person to sit perfectly still for 60 seconds or more while the camera shutter remained open. It was during this time that Mumler's assistant would put on a flowing robe, sneak in behind the person having their picture taken and remain there for only about 10 to 20 seconds. Then the assistant would move out of the shot unbeknownst to the person having their picture taken. Once the picture was developed, a semi-transparent apparition would appear. Other effects used by Mumler were simple double-exposures. Despite the fact that Mumler was a fake, he did bring the subject of spirit photography into the limelight in the late 19th century.

Spirit photography had become a fad during the 1890s and even though some were charlatans, there were other photographers capturing unexplained images without trickery. As cameras and photographic techniques became more advanced photographers began to realize that some of the photos being taken in haunted places could not be explained or attributed to film flaws or lighting effects.

Captain Provand, a professional photographer, was taking pictures of Raynham Hall in Norfolk, England, for a magazine assignment. While he was taking some shots inside the house his assistant looked up and saw an apparition of a woman coming down the stairs. She immediately had Provand take the shots of this event as it unfolded before them. When he developed the film, to their amazement, they had captured a hooded female figure coming down the stairs and this famous photo is now referred to as the "Brown Lady." For years the photo has been examined many times with no explanation of what could have caused such a shape.

For the past 100 years cameras, equipment and technology have continued to improve greatly. Even with this advancement photos can still be faked and that's why it is so important to follow a strict scientific method when performing spirit photography.

Cameras Used as a Medium

Spirit photography is an aid to mediumship. By using the camera we allow the spirits to communicate with us instead of us, communicating with them. As you continue to use your camera to take pictures of spirits your results will continue to improve with each investigation. When I started developing my group of ghost hunters, I took them to places where I had prior success capturing paranormal images in my photos. I would use one or two rolls of film and get six to twelve great photos with different anomalous shapes. At first the others in the group would take twice as many pictures as I would and not get a thing in their photos that would indicate ghosts. I explained to them that the same thing happened to me and as the spirits became more comfortable with me and I became more knowledgeable of the spirit world I started having greater success with my photos capturing ghosts forms. It didn't take long for my team members to start getting good results. Now, this is not to say this happens to everyone. Sometimes the first time out you will get great results with your spirit photography. I just want you to know that if you don't get anything the first couple of times you try, don't give up. It will happen. As we raise our awareness we come to understand that there is evidence of intelligent forms of energy we associate with as ghosts or spirits.

If I'm asked what is the best camera, best film or speed of film to use during an investigation, I tell them what works best for me. Once you get started you may decide that something else works better for you. This does not mean that I'm right and you are wrong or you're right and I'm wrong. It just means we have different ways to achieve the same goal. As far as a camera goes, you can get good results with everything from expensive $1,000, 35 mm cameras and digitals to cheap disposable ones.

When it comes to film speed, I prefer Kodak 200 or 400 for inside shots and 800 or 1000 for outside shots. Once you get out there taking pictures on your own, you will soon learn what works better for you. I feel more comfortable using four different types of cameras. I have a digital Nikon 900 series that is a phenomenal camera, a great Nikon 35 mm, a mid-range-priced Cannon 35 mm, and an inexpensive 35 mm from Polaroid. I use my digital Nikon camera as my tracker. I start my photography session with my digital and as soon as I pick up any anomalies, I alert the team members to where I'm getting paranormal shots. Most of the time I'll get the same type of shapes in the same area with my 35 mm camera.

You will hear a lot of controversy among ghost hunters about the use of the digital camera. It seems that when they first came out there was a problem with the performance and as a result, you would get orbs resulting from an imperfection in the workings of the digital. Over the last few years these camera companies have made wonderful advancements, so if you have a more current digital, the problem may not exist. Until I can be sure of this, I still rely on my 35 mm for photographic evidence, because I can show a negative for further examination to a claim of paranormal anomalies. If I use my digital camera and get the same shots from my 35 mm cameras along with other results that there is paranormal activity going on, then I use my digital pictures to add to my credible evidence.

Paranormal Anomalies in Photos

1) **Orbs** are globe-shaped lights of energy caught on film. Orbs represent the life-force energy patterns of an individual who has died. They are made up of the life force that powered its human body. I have been asked why the spirits take the shape of an orb. If a spirit could form a barrier around its energy (as in a bubble), the energy would gently push against all sides equally, causing an orb shape. The spirit may also have control over the size and density. Some of my photos have shown where the orbs will join together to form a large orb in moments of distress, or unite for strength. Weather plays an

important part while taking pictures of a haunted area. If it is raining, snowing or the wind is blowing up dust, these elements can interfere and produce orb-like anomalies in your photos.

2) **A vortex** is a small tornado-shaped image that shows up on photos when there is a spirit or spirits present. You can see the orbs rotating inside the shaft. Sometimes the vortex is so dense that it will cast a shadow. It is believed that the vortex is a means of travel for the spirits from our world to the next. The orb pattern in a vortex suggests a barrier oscillation effect resulting in an orb entering our physical domain vibrating at a higher rate compared to our physical domain. The barrier oscillation effect occurs when a spirit orb enters our barrier still vibrating at a higher vibrational frequency.

3) **Ectoplasmic Mist** can show up in photos, varying in different shades of gray, green, white, black and red, which were not present when the photo was taken. These strange mists show up in the photos as some kind of paranormal energy. Take precautions that you are not photographing fog, moisture, exhaust, smoke, or your own breath when the air is cold.

4) **Human Form** is the most rare of all the ghost pictures taken. It is so easy to fake an apparition photo with all the latest technology. Because of this, it gets harder for the ghost hunter to prove when an apparition really shows up in a photo.

I had just come out of the cemetery at Colonial Williamsburg and asked the ghosts for permission to take a photo of them with me. This is a very heavy ectoplasmic mist with a shield forming down on the left side. You can see the tree clearly through the mist, so the picture is not out of focus.

This is a Christmas picture of me and my daughter, Ashley Highsmith, with my sister, Wanda Belcher, and her husband Bob and her two daughters Nichole and Ginger. It was the first time we had all been together for Christmas since our mom had died. I feel like it was mom's chance to let us know that she was enjoying the reunion. Notice the top of the vortex and you can see the orbs traveling within the tube shapes made up in the vortex. No, there is not a lamp in front of the camera that could have made this anomaly appear.

This is Evelyn Schmidt playing her violin, in her Bloomfield home and the anomaly is a vortex. Her mom, Melody Schmidt, feels that it is her dad visiting whenever Evelyn plays her beautiful music. This photo was taken by Melody Schmidt.

Sometimes during an investigation of a haunted place I will get a dark ectoplasmic mist instead of a white mist. This photo was taken at the Jailer's Inn in Bardstown, Kentucky, where we were able to capture a few friendly ghosts in our photos as orbs and mists. This photo was taken by Chuck Starr.

This is a very unusual anomaly, like one I've never seen before. Notice the shadow of the tentacles on the person's arm as he sleeps. This was sent to me by Shoshanna Gross.

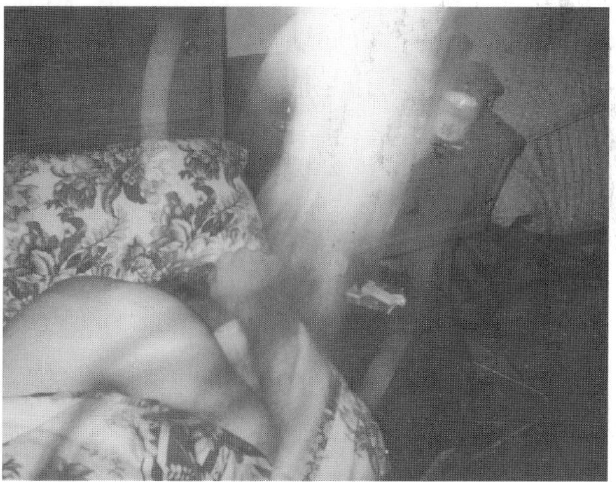

My husband took me to meet his father shortly after we were married. His mom had passed away 7 years earlier and his dad was 93 years old. When I sat down and started to play his mom's piano I got a sensation that she was there and happy that Chuck had remarried. I asked Chuck to take my picture to see if we would get anything in our photo and we got this beautiful orb. Photo taken by Chuck Starr.

While at the Mansion at Marriott's Griffin Gate Resort, Chuck took this photo just after we recorded the little girl's message,"Daddy was causing the lights." When I took a magnifying glass I could see the face of a little girl in the mat of the picture hanging behind the employee. Photo taken by Chuck Starr.

(below right) In a plantation home in Bloomfield, Kentucky, we were doing an investigation in an area of the house once known as the slave quarters. While filming this area with a Sony nightshot camcorder we were able to capture many flying orbs. I was also lucky enough to get many of them on my digital camera and four other 35 mm cameras. We also got a voice on our Sony nightshot that says, "Coffee, coffee," as one of the orbs flies across the room. Chuck had just asked the owners if he could have a cup of coffee when we captured the ghost voice. This photo was taken by Patti Starr.

Chapter 20

Moon Phases & Ghost Hunting

"I shall not commit the fashionable stupidity of regarding everything I cannot explain as fraud."
C.G. Jung, 1819

The moon is primarily made up of rock with a minor iron core. Its exterior is covered in a powdery blanket called the lunar regolith, a blend of loose rocks and very fine dust. The moon is geologically almost completely dead and has essentially no atmosphere or weather. Its properties record nearly the entire history of the solar system. Comparable to most of the other satellites, the moon has become locked in to synchronize its revolution around the earth encircling in a slightly elliptical orbit at 2,300 miles per hour.

In general, when most of us talk about the moon we identify eight different phases. They are the new, waxing crescent, first quarter, waxing gibbous, full, waning gibbous, last quarter, and waning crescent.

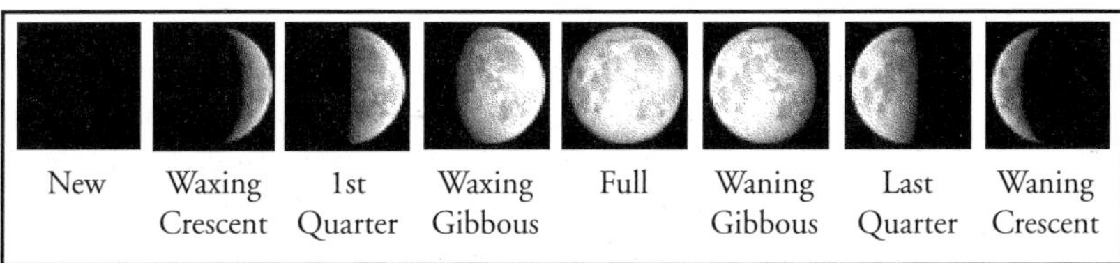

Interesting facts about the Moon

1) It takes about twenty-nine and a half days for the moon to complete one cycle.

2) The phase of the moon is determined by the relative positions of the earth, moon and sun, so the phase of the moon is the same for everyone everywhere on earth.

3) Each phase of the moon will rise at a different time. The full moon rises at sunset. Each night, after that it will come up about 48 minutes later. The new moon is the hardest to see because it rises around the same time as the sun.

4) When we look at the full moon, it seems to stay full for a few days. This is because of the geometry of the way the light from the sun falls on the moon and is observed by us here on earth. The full moon and new moon seem to last longer than the other phases. But, in fact, the moon is at any particular phase for just an instant, like noon, it happens and then it is past. This optical illusion probably contributes to many myths about things being more likely to happen when the moon is full.

5) The moon may impact different things on earth. The tug of the moon and sun can affect the oceans, giving us high and low tides. The light of a full moon can be very bright, affecting animal hunting habits. The full moon has been blamed from more babies being born in a single night and for some one losing their mind during a lunar cycle, thus the word lunatic.

6) The blue moon term comes from an old folklore explaining that when you have two full moons in one month it is called a "Blue Moon." This is also believed to be where the expression, "Once in a blue moon", comes from. The term

has been around for over 400 years, but the calendar reference has become more popular over the last 20 years.

During my research of ghost hunting I've noted that paranormal activity seems to be more heightened three days before, during and three days after a full moon and new moon. The phases of the moon seem to affect not only many things on earth, but also some subjects of the paranormal. Early psychologists had no doubt about the moon's effect on our mental states. During the full moon the lunatics in the asylums would be separated from the chronically insane, and extra staff were scheduled. The word "lunatic," is a derivative of the Latin word "Luna."

The Ghosts Asked Us to Come Back

Chuck and I, along with my group of students from Lexington Community College, went to an abandoned tuberculosis hospital in Kentucky, three days before a new moon. The solar weather conditions were also a plus with active sun flares and unsettled geomagnetic fields. I felt sure that these conditions would contribute to our success in getting EVPs and anomalies in our photos and videos. The state hospital opened its doors in the 1950s during the time when so many people were dying of tuberculosis. The highly contagious bacterial infection required that patients be quarantined. The building has been vacant for about 20 years. It has four floors and is in severe disrepair. The majority of the windows throughout the building were broken out and glass was everywhere.

We were very reverent and said our prayers before entering the abandoned building. We announced ourselves and told the spirits that we were not going to make fun of them or in any way hurt them. We also explained that we were there to prove that they existed and we asked them to please speak to us and give us permission to photograph them. As soon as we began to get orbs with our digital cameras we thanked them. Then we alerted the others to the active area and they also started getting the same results, with orbs showing up on their cameras and video recorders.

These were orbs captured with a digital camera at the abandoned TB hospital in Kentucky by Rhea Clark. She is a psychic who joined our investigation for that evening. She also picked up a feeling of a little girl's presence before we even knew we had her voice saying, "Mommy" and "I've been sittin' here all day" on our recorders.

We got some wonderful footage with flying orbs on the nightshot, lots of orbs in photos, and some great voices on our audio recorders. Our modest Gauss EMF meter kept going off and we were thrilled, since there are no electrical currents, telephone wires, or cables going through the building that would have caused the meter to go off. Each time the meter went off we either got a voice or captured an orb on digital camera and video.

After making our nightshot camcorder stationary, I decided to dowse and while walking down the dark, musky, hallway I was pushed and fell against the opposite wall. It didn't frighten me it just felt like someone was trying to get my attention. I continued following the lead of the dowsing rods and ended up in what looked like a treatment room. Once my rods crossed, I realized I had a spirit that was willing to communicate with us. I started with my standard yes and no questions, to find out if I was talking to a male or female, what age they were, when they died, and so on. Once I had most of this information, I asked this male ghost if he was the one that pushed me in the hall and the rods responded to yes. When I got home and listened to the audio from my mini recorder that I was wearing during my dowsing, I got a male voice that said, "Yes." I had invited two psychics, Jason Lewis and Rhea Clark, to come along with me while I dowsed. During the questioning session I asked them if they had thought of a name. Jason asked the ghost, "Does your name start with a 'D,' is it David, is that what it is?" Immediately after this question we got another "Yes," from the same voice. Of course, we did not hear the voices during the questioning but we managed to capture them on the audiotapes.

We went down to the morgue to see if we could record anything and filmed an orb flying right to left in the middle of the room. We were a little uncomfortable there so decided to go on down the hall. We went into the x-ray room and around some of the tables and shelving we were able to capture more orbs on our digital and in our nightshot. Just as we were leaving this area we were fortunate to get a little girl's voice on my audiocassette, as did five other students on their audio recorders. She says, "I've been sittin' here all day." It is a very clear EVP and there were no children with us during the entire investigation. Once we were home and I viewed the nightshot film, I was pleased that we got a flying orb around us, and the little girl's voice at the same time. Later on, as we traveled down the hall, we also picked up her voice again and she cries out, "Mommy." It's a very sad sounding EVP.

While Bill Scott, another member of the group, was up on the fourth floor alone, he sneezed and captured on audio and nightshot film a male voice saying, "Bless you." At one point, in a very dark area I said, "I get so turned around," and just after I said that a male voice on the recorder says, "Bless you." It sounded different from the voice Bill had captured earlier, so we don't think it was coming from the same source.

In another room that I had ventured into alone, I was able to pick up a couple of EVPs that said, "Help me, help me," and one that was very desperate-sounding and said, "Help, me, please!" Since I don't get to hear these messages until I'm at home listening to my audio recordings, it makes me feel sad that I didn't get a chance to say

This is a picture taken during an investigation at the abandoned TB hospital in Kentucky. We were able to get moving orbs in several shots with our Sony nightshot camcorder. With our digital and 35 mm cameras we captured orbs around Bill Scott in different locations of the hospital. This photo was taken by Patti Starr.

something to the ghosts that might have made them feel better.

At one point in the evening we were laughing and cutting up a little to release some of the nervous energy from such a stressful investigation and I thought it was really funny that during that part of the investigation I picked up another EVP that says, "Quiet," and it reminded me of being a little too loud in a hospital and having the nurse come up to tell you to be, "Quiet."

While Bill Scott was on the fourth floor, checking out the building for vagrants to make sure it was safe before starting the investigation, Jason was on the third floor doing the same thing. Jason was checking in with Bill on the walkie-talkie, to see if all was clear. Just after Bill answered Jason, Bill picked up a male voice that says very clearly, "It did not break it."

The best moving orb, of all the many orbs we were able to

film, was the one that followed Bill down the hall as he went to gather his equipment as we were getting ready to leave the site. He stepped out in front of our nightshot, which was focused down the hall, and walked by with his nightshot in his hand, recording as he walked. Within a few seconds a brilliant solid orb flew by our camera, down the hall behind Bill, flew around him and then came flying back towards us and passed our camera. At that point, Bill turned around and asked if anyone had flashed the thermal scanner or a flashlight down his way. We told him we were busy packing and that no one was near the thermal scanner or flashlight. Lucky for us we were able to capture the same orb on two different nightshot camcorders from two different angles.

When Bill had not returned as quickly as we thought he should, Jason called down to see if he was coming back, but got no answer. We could hear movement, but we still could not see Bill. We became concerned and Jason called out again. By now, Jason was starting to go down the hall to see what is holding Bill up and Jason's wife Susan pleaded with him not to go. For a few moments we all began feeling a bit more anxious and the unknown fear was about to set in and distort our reality. Finally, in the far distance we saw Bill's flashlight and he motioned to us that it was him. We were so relieved. During this scare we picked up an EVP that was the most frightening sound of them all. I'm glad that we didn't hear it while we were waiting for Bill or we may have run out screaming. The EVP we recorded was in a rough monotone and it said in a demanding way, "Tell us," and it didn't even sound human.

As we concluded our investigation we all met outside the building, held hands and said a prayer of thanks and asked for protection as we asked the ghosts not to follow us home. As I was packing the equipment away in the trunk of our car, I got one more EVP that says, "Come back." What a perfect ending to a perfect investigation.

Chapter 21

Paranormal Terminology

"Death is as sure for that which is born,
as birth is for that which is dead.
Therefore grieve not for what is inevitable."

Bhagavad-Gita

Agent is the human being that sees the ghost or apparition.
Altered State of Consciousness is any state of consciousness who differs from the normal states of being awake or asleep.
Amulet is an article that has the power to stave off ghosts and evil spirits.
Angels are a holy and protective messengers shielding us from harm. They are sometimes mistaken for ghosts.
Apparition is a mysterious image of a disembodied spirit that can be recognized as a human or animal or object. They are the most rare type of ghost to capture on film. Ghostly human forms are the easiest to fake, especially with the advanced technology of computers. This makes it even more difficult to prove apparitions when using photos. Ghostly apparitions of ships, trains, cars, and other inanimate objects have been seen.
Apport happens when a solid object appears from out of nowhere, with the assistance of the spirit in the company of a medium.
Astral Plane is a level of awareness in the celestial world having its own standards, occupants, and reason for being.
Astral Body is the energy that separates itself from the human form but still maintains the personality and feelings of the individual. Sometimes others will see them during their Out-of-Body Experience (OBE) or Near-Death Experience (NDE).
Atmospheric Apparition is a visual imprint the person who has died left on the atmosphere, that continues to replay.
Aura is an energy field that surrounds all living things.
Automatic Writing happens when a ghost or spirit takes control of the writer's hand and writes out a message
Banshee is a spirit that appears prior to a person's death to howl a mourning song and to welcome them into the afterlife.
Bi-location is the phenomena where someone can be in two places at the same time.
Boogie Man is the term that children refer to when they believe they have someone or something in their closet or under their bed.
Cemetery lights are bluish balls of lights that have been sighted after dark hovering over graves.
Channeling is a form of spirit possession with a medium while communicating for wisdom or future events with the unseen entity.
Clairaudience is when someone has the

ability to hear the voices of ghosts and other sounds that are inaudible to the human ear.

Clairvoyance is being capable of seeing events in the future or past through the mind's eye.

Cold Reading is done when a psychic has no prior knowledge of the sitter.

Cold Spot is an area in the haunted premises where the temperature drops by several degrees. The temperature can also rise in heat by several degrees indicating a possible fire in the past.

Collective Apparition happens when more than one living person sights a ghost or spirit at the some time.

Collective Unconscious was a term to describe a form of analytical psychology developed by Carl Jung. It represents the collective memory of all humanity's past and is held somewhere inside the unconscious mind.

Conjure is an act to summon a spirit to manifest itself for a desired task or to answer questions.

Corpse candle is a term referring to the balls of fire lights that dance above the ground.

Crisis Apparition is the vision of someone that will appear during waking hours or in a dream at the moment of a crisis.

Dowsing is the ability to seek answers and interpret them by using rods or a pendulum. Dowsing is widely used as a simple, but effective, way of searching for anything from lost coins, water, and geophysical surveys to ghosts.

Earthlights are balls of lights or variable patches of lights appearing randomly and with no explanation as to what causes them.

Ectoplasm is a solid or vaporous substance, which is produced by a medium during a trance to reach the deceased. Most reports of ectoplasm were revealed to be hoaxs. The medium would take cheesecloth and rig it to drop from a part of the body (the nose, mouth or ears). Some mediums even swallowed the cheesecloth and then regurgitated it later on during the séance.

Ectoplasmic Mist will usually show up in a photo as a misty white cloud to indicate the presence of a spirit. The mist is not seen when the picture is taken. These mists can vary in color from gray, black, red and green.

Elemental Spirit is one that is associated with one of the four elements, fire, air, water, and earth.

EMF (Electro-Magnetic Field) meter is a device that can pick up electronic and magnetic fields. It can detect any distortions in the normal electromagnetic field.

Entity is a term that refers to an intelligent being who is no longer inside the physical body. They have the power to provide information to all individuals who are sensitive to their vibrations.

ESP (Extrasensory Perception) is a condition where one has the ability to gather information beyond the five human senses.

EVP (Electrical Voice Phenomenon or Electrical Visual Phenomenon) is a method in which you can pick up a spirit's voice by means of audiocassette recorder or any other recording device. It is also possible to pick up visual images of a known dead person coming through computers and televisions when they are not on.

Exorcism is a method used by priests or other qualified individuals to withdraw offending spirits from people and places to which the spirits have attached themselves.

Exorcist is the individual who is skilled in removing the demon from within. This ceremony is usually performed by a religious "holy man."

Fairy is a tiny, human-like winged mythical being. The pranks they play are sometimes mistaken for the activities of ghosts or poltergeists. Many types of fairies are believed to exist with each one being connected to an element, as in earth (gnomes), fire (salamanders), air (sylphs), and water (undines).

Family Apparition is a ghost that haunts one particular family. When the ghost appears, it is an omen that someone in the family is going to die.

Ghosts are different forms of apparitions

of deceased human spirits that can appear to any of our five senses. They can be seen as shadowy human or animal form. They can be heard and even emit a familiar or offensive odors. They are trapped between worlds.

Ghost Catcher is a type of wind chime that will clink together as ghosts wisp by.

Ghost Hunt consists of a conscious effort to search out a known ghost or visit other places suspected to be haunted.

Ghost Investigation involves going into an area looking for ghosts or haunting under controlled conditions. Reports are made to document the events. Listing all the readings of the equipment along with time, weather, and temperature as the project unfolds, becomes valuable information for the research.

Ghost Hunter is a person who seeks to find ghosts or haunted places to figure out why, or what type of spirit activity is occurring.

Ghost Buster is experienced in clearing an area of the ghosts, poltergeists, spirits or other haunted activity.

Ghoul is a grotesque, evil spirit that robs a grave to eat the flesh of the recent dead.

Gray Lady is a reference used to describe the ghost of a woman who has been murdered by her lover or one who waits for the return of a loved one.

Haunt is the place where the ghost or spirit continues to return. Ghosts usually haunt places and not people.

Haunting is the repeated display of paranormal activity in a designated area. Some hauntings are thought to be poltergeist energy from a disembodied entity trapped in a certain location or by the energy left behind from a very strong tragic event or accident. Occasionally, hauntings appear to be an intelligent ghost trying to make a connection with someone on the earth plane to give a message.

Ley Lines is an area where invisible lines run between sacred objects or locations.

Luminous Body is a term referring to a faint glow in a dead body to signify a soul's pending departure.

Malevolent Entities are spirits that are very angry or seeking revenge. They sometimes attach themselves to someone causing them discomfort and distress. It is easy for them to harass human beings with the same angry or depressed personality.

Medium is someone who can communicate with the dead. During a trance state, the medium allows the spirit to take over his or her body so he can deliver a message to the living. The medium does not remember any of this once he comes out of the trance. Today the new mediums are referred to as channelers. The big difference is that now the medium remains completely conscious of what he says and experiences through the spirit.

NDE (Near-Death Experience) is when a person dies and is revived after a short period of time. The person remembers the death experience and visions of the afterlife, which include ghosts and other paranormal events. Survivors of this experience say it changes their whole outlook on death and they feel they can live better lives from this realization.

Necromancer is a person considered to be a sorcerer or wizard, who has the power to raise the dead and force the spirits to obtain information about the future.

Orbs are globe-shaped lights of energy caught on film, usually during a haunting or other paranormal experience. Orbs are believed to represent the spirit of an individual who has died. They are made up of the life force that powered their body in life. They may vary in size, color, and density.

Omen is a foretelling of a future event.

Oracle is a prophet who can communicate with spirits, ghosts, and gods to obtain information.

Ouija Board is a board with numbers, alphabet, and the words "yes," "no," and "good-bye," printed on the surface. It comes with a planchette (a pointer) and once you lightly place your hand on it the pointer will spell out the answers to the questions asked by the players. This game of the Ouija Board can be dangerous if you are unaware of what you are doing and not educated in psychic science.

Paranormal is any experience that happens beyond the range of scientific explanation or normal human capabilities. These experiences may include hauntings, telekinesis, telepathy, clairvoyance, or any other rarity that cannot be justified by the five senses.

Planchette is a pointer used with a Ouija Board to communicate with spirits, ghosts, or entities of a higher plane.

Poltergeist is a noisy and sometimes violent spirit. The name "Poltergeist" has Greek roots meaning "noisy ghost." Known actions of the poltergeist are banging, thumping, moving objects, levitating, and causing fires. These same actions can also be due to an unconscious outburst of psychokinesis. More researchers of today feel that a lot of poltergeist activity is related to psychokinesis, rather than ghosts.

Possession is when an evil entity takes over a human body and forces the soul out. This allows the spirit to use the host by alternating his own will. This may totally adjust the host's current personality. The people most commonly attacked by this force are women under twenty who show signs of emotional distress. The disincarnate spirit seeks out humans with their own emotions of anger, revenge, and resentment.

Precognition is the foreknowing of future events.

Psychic is a person who tunes into phenomena beyond their five senses. The talents of a psychic include, but are not limited to, hearing voices, seeing spirits and knowing what might be happening in the future. Unfortunately, these gifts have been misinterpreted as a mental illness for some. Psychics have also been referred to as seers or sensitives.

Psychokinesis is the ability to move objects with the power of the mind only.

Purgatory is the place where the souls of the dead must go to be cleansed of all their sins before being allowed into heaven, according to Catholicism.

Reciprocal Apparition is an experience where both the individual and ghost see and react to each other.

Reincarnation is a belief that once a person dies, his soul returns to a new body where it will continue its lessons about life and how to reach enlightenment. Many reincarnations may be necessary for the soul to learn and become closer to the goal of perfection.

Retrocognition is the foreknowing of past events.

Scrying is a form of divination in which an individual stares deeply into an object in order to see an image that might appear. This object could be a mirror, crystal ball, or a flame. The images that appear can be symbolic and give answers to a question. A spirit usually generates these images.

Séance consists of a group of people sitting in a circle holding hands in hope of contacting the dead. The procedure is conducted by a medium who goes into a trance and is used as a vehicle for the deceased spirit to take over and communicate with their loved ones.

Sensitive refers to a person who can detect paranormal events beyond the range of his five senses.

Shaman is a medicine man or witch doctor who can communicate with the spirits during a trance and who also possesses the power of healing.

Sixth Sense is to have the power of perception in addition to the five senses. It is also a popular term for extrasensory perception (ESP).

Smudging is a form of cleansing or the clearing of a spirit from an area by using incense to purify the area.

Spirit Guide is a heavenly spirit or guardian angel that is present and offers help to the person to whom it is attached. This help may be a simple hunch or a certain feeling that comes over the person who needs guidance for a problem or situation. Some people claim that they can communicate with their guides at all times.

Spirit Photography is usually a photo that contains a face or form believed to be that of a deceased person.

Spiritualism is a belief structure that spirits and ghosts can communicate with the living.

Supernatural is when an unexplained occurrence take place out of the realm of the known forces of nature. The experience usually involves spirits.

Table-tipping (Typology) is a type of communication with the spirit world through the use of a table. You start out with any size table and surround it with a number of people. Everyone places all five fingers lightly on the table. All together the group chants, "Table up, Table up." Usually the table will start to quiver or lift to one side. If someone in the group has strong energy, the table might rock back and forth or lift off the floor. At this point, a question may be asked with a response from the table tapping once for "yes" and two for "no." If there is a nonbeliever present, the table will probably not move. This type of entertainment can be dangerous and is not recommended to those unskilled in psychic science.

Telekinesis is where a person can move an object through the power of thought without physical means to move the object.

Telepathy is a method of communication from mind to mind. Dr. Rhine of Duke University proved that the mind could communicate with other minds and successfully transmit information.

Teleportation happens when an object can be transported from one location to another by disappearing and then reappearing in a different place, even going through solid objects.

Time Slips occur when the past and present collide at a location.

Transmigration is a belief that a soul can move from body to body through the process of reincarnation.

Vassage is a spirit that inhabits a scrying crystal. During the session, the spirit communicates by forming literal or symbolic images.

Vortex is a small tornado-shape image that shows up on pictures when there is a spirit present. You can see the orbs rotating inside the shaft. Sometimes the vortex is so dense that it will cast a shadow. It is believed that the vortex is a means of travel for the spirits in the orb form.

Will-o'-the-Wisp is a ball of flame that floats in mid air. They have also been observed bobbing or dancing just above the ground in yellow and blue flames. These wondrous episodes have been recorded since Roman times. The Native Americans believed them to be fire spirits warning everyone of danger. The Germans thought the balls of flames were lost or trapped souls that couldn't move on. In Africa, some believed that the Will-o'-the-Wisp was witches trying to scare sinners into behaving properly. In Russia, these lights represent the souls of stillborn infants. Throughout Europe, when these lights appeared it was thought to be evil spirits that couldn't enter heaven, but were not evil enough to be condemned to hell.